BEFORE WILFRID

BRITONS, ROMANS AND ANGLO-SAXONS IN TYNEDALE

Edited by Tom Corfe

Hexham Local History Society
1997

ISSN 1363-0563
ISBN 0 9527615 1 3
© Hexham Local History Society and Contributors
Printed by Robson Print Ltd, Hexham

The *Hexham Historian* is an annual publication which usually includes a miscellany of articles relating to Hexham and Tynedale. This special issue is confined to one topic, which formed the basis for a conference arranged by Hexham Local History Society in November 1996.

CONTRIBUTORS

Paul Bidwell is Principal Keeper (Archaeology) of Tyne and Wear Museums, based at Arbeia Roman Fort and Museum, South Shields. He has excavated throughout the North-East, and also in Devon. His books include reports on *Vindolanda* (1985) and (with Neil Holbrook) *Hadrian's Wall Bridges* (1989).

Tom Corfe was a teacher and lecturer who now edits *Hexham Historian*. His books include *Hexham Heritage* (1991).

Rosemary Cramp was Professor of Archaeology at the University of Durham. Her excavations include Monkwearmouth and Jarrow. Among many publications, she has edited Volume I (Durham and Northumberland) of the British Academy's *Corpus of Anglo-Saxon Stone Sculpture* (1984).

Jim Crow lectures in archaeology at the University of Newcastle. He has directed many excavations on Hadrian's Wall, where he worked for the National Trust, and is currently busy at High Rochester. His books include *Housesteads* (1995).

Margaret Snape is on the staff of Tyne and Wear Museums at Arbeia Roman Fort. She has excavated at a number of Roman and post-Roman sites, and has published articles on many aspects of Roman archaeology.

Tony Wilmott is an archaeologist for English Heritage who has excavated all over the country, and directed six years of excavations at Birdoswald. His report on the fort is about to be published.

CONTENTS

1. STARTING POINTS	5.
2. THE ROMANS IN TYNEDALE Jim Crow and Tom Corfe	10
3. ROMAN ROADS AND BRIDGES IN TYNEDALE Paul Bidwell	18
4. THE AFTERMATH OF ROME Tony Wilmott	29
5. AN ANGLO-SAXON WATERMILL AT CORBRIDGE Margaret Snape	40
6. BERNICIA BEFORE WILFRID Tom Corfe and Rosemary Cramp	57
7. THE BATTLE OF HEAVENFIELD Tom Corfe	65
8. HEXHAM BEFORE WILFRID?	87
Index	94

MAPS AND ILLUSTRATIONS

1.1 The Roman North: Roads and Bridges	4
2.1 Broomhouse Common Settlement	10
2.2 A Roman wine-strainer from Whitfield	10
2.3 Roman Tynedale	12
3.1 The second Roman bridge at Chesters	25
5.1 Corstopitum, general site plan, 1907	40
5.2 Corbridge Roman site	44
5.3 Corbridge, Armstrong map, 1769	46
5.4 The Tyne near Corbridge, Fryer's map, 1820	46
5.5 Corbridge and environs, 1778, from John Fryer's map	48
5.6 Corbridge Open Fields	50
5.7 Colchester Field in 1776	51
5.8 Tamworth Anglo-Saxon watermill: reconstructed section	53
5.9 The Anglo-Saxon watermill at Corbridge	54
6.1 Northumbria in the seventh century	58
6.2 Anglo-Saxon sites in Northumberland and Durham	60
7.1 Heavenfield: St. Oswald's Church and the roadside Cross	67
7.2 Heavenfield and Rowley Burn	78
7.3 Rheged and Northumbria, c590-634	80
7.4 Northern Dynasties	82
8.1 Roman roads in Tynedale, after Selkirk	91

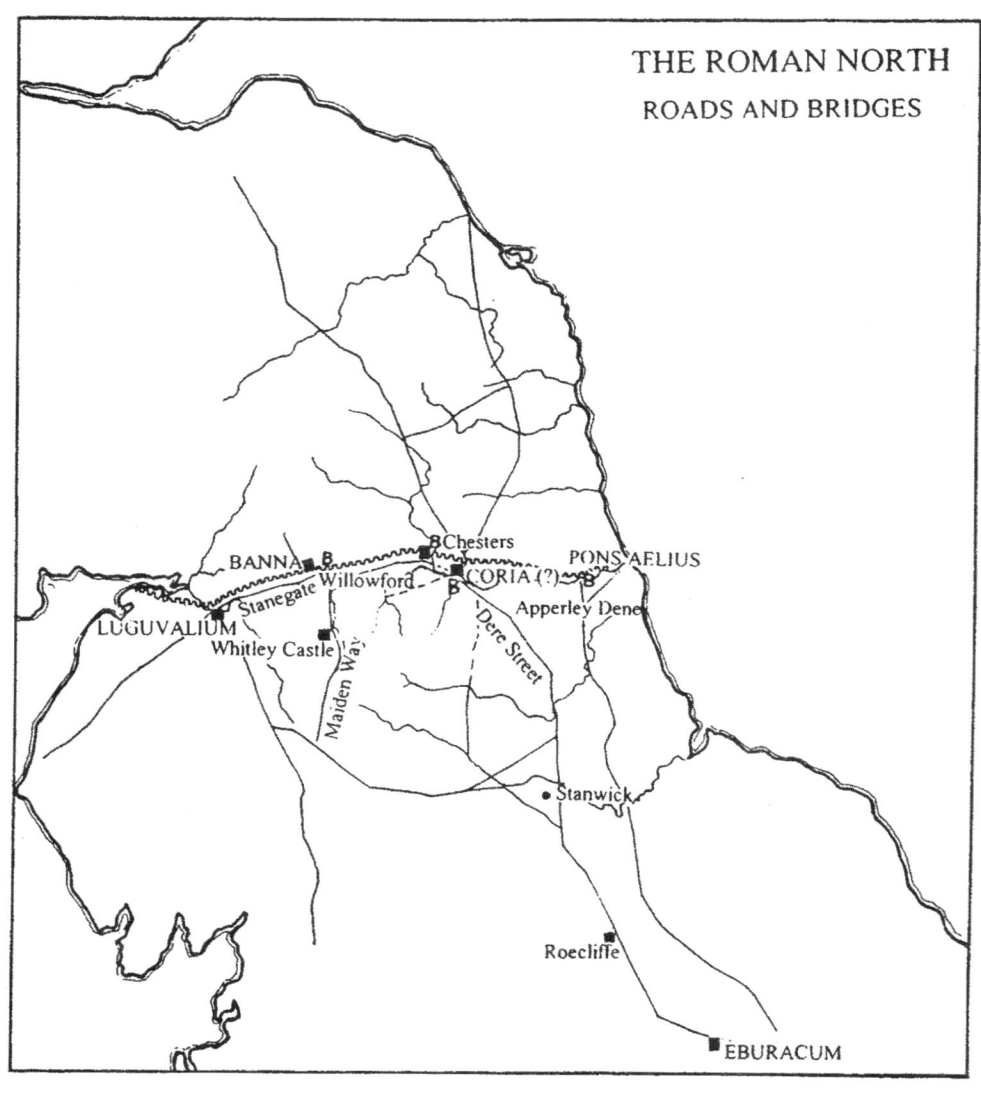

1. STARTING POINTS

History begins in Tynedale soon after 670. Bede and Stephanus tell the story of Aethelthryth of Northumbria, whose preference for the intellectual and spiritual life of the cloister led her to forsake husband and kingdom. Before departing she granted to her mentor Bishop Wilfrid an estate that is generally identified with the medieval Hexhamshire (Colgrave & Mynors 1969, 390-397; Colgrave 1927, 42-5; Kirby 1974, 1969-171).

Any attempt to understand what happened in Tynedale before Wilfrid's arrival depends heavily upon archaeological evidence, and upon interpretation of the few and late historical sources, supplemented by occasional clues from such other disciplines as the study of place-names. In November 1996 seven people well acquainted with this evidence met at Hexham, and were joined by some two hundred others in pooling knowledge and views. This is a version of the main contributions and conclusions. All who took part have either provided copies of their papers, or have generously helped the editor to produce a summary of what was said.

There is a huge bulk of archaeological evidence relating to the Roman period in the North, though focussed on the military frontier of Hadrian's Wall rather than in rural Tynedale behind it. Roman military occupation was imposed upon an area of mixed farming. The stony ridges north of the Tyne are dotted with very visible remains of Iron Age settlements and fields, including a major hillfort at Warden; but there is only scanty evidence of the similar occupation in the valley itself, while the Shire south of the Tyne is largely an archaeological blank. Local tribal allegiance is obscure: to the north were the Votadini, to the south the Brigantian confederacy, but just where the two met is uncertain. Other local groups are hinted at, each in a single inscription (one of them now lost): the Corionototae and Textoverdi (Collingwood & Wright 1965, nos 1142 and 1695; Rivet & Smith 1979, 322, 329, 470-2). We know little about society, economy or political divisions in Tynedale, the density of population or state of the landscape. Nor do we know anything of the local considerations that may have influenced Rome in settling its frontier hereabouts.

The processes of Roman conquest are perhaps most clearly seen at Corbridge Site Museum. It has material from the first fort established there about AD 86, and from the earlier Red House supply base set up nearby under Agricola, perhaps about AD 79 (Bishop & Dore 1988, 3, 126-9, 140; Hanson et al 1979). How much opposition Rome faced, initially and throughout the occupation, is uncertain. So is how the region adapted and developed under Roman rule. We cannot be sure whether Tynedale farmers settled down to a life of peace, prosperity and friendly commerce with the military establishment that was only occasionally disrupted by troublemakers; or if they spent three hundred years sullenly resenting a foreign yoke and seething with frustration. What is certainly clear is that the occupation early laid out a basic road system with related forts. That road pattern led directly to the development of a fixed frontier by the AD 120s (Breeze & Dobson 1976 11-27; Breeze 1982, 36-96, 161-70). Into this widely accepted story, Raymond Selkirk has thrown several spanners by suggesting an elaborate Roman road network south and east of Hexham (Selkirk 1995, 98; see pp 91-3 below).

The Hadrian's Wall system has been thoroughly studied. So have the fort and vicus at Vindolanda, and the supply base at Corbridge. But the effect of the Wall on the rural areas behind it is less clear. There has been little examination of Romano-British farming in this area, little discussion of the continuity or change it reflected, or of the relations of occupiers and natives, of tribal communities and military administration. Such relations presumably changed very considerably over three centuries, and we can detect something of this in the civil settlements established at Vindolanda and Corbridge. We glimpse from the Vindolanda letters the contempt with which, in the early days, Roman soldiers regarded the *Brittunculi*. We observe from surviving inscriptions that they nevertheless made efforts to humour native religious beliefs, to the extent of syncretizing local deities with their own. Built into the crypt at Hexham is a recycled altar to 'Apollo Maponus' (Collingwood & Wright 1965, no 1122). Beyond that, we know little of Romanisation outside the urban settlements. Did Tynedale farmers embrace Roman culture and prosper from Roman commerce? Were they affected by military and civil influences from distant parts of the Empire? These and related questions are among those touched on here by Jim Crow and Paul Bidwell, who have between them dug the length and breadth of Roman Tynedale; though even that has not produced definitive answers.

One particularly irritating gap in our understanding of Roman Tynedale relates to Hexham itself. Evidence for a permanent settlement on the site has been long

1. STARTING POINTS

sought and much debated. While no proof has ever been found for such a settlement, and no arguments have swayed scholarly opinion in favour of the idea, it remains impossible to prove the negative view. This is the question that first triggered the enquiry, so this book closes with a survey of the evidence for what might have happened on the site of Hexham before Wilfrid's arrival.

The Roman occupation seems to have come to an end in the northern frontier zone of Britain between 367 and 410. At this point we face the most uncertain period in the history of the North. There has been much speculation about the successor communities and their way of life. The nearest relevant archaeological information comes from just outside Tynedale, from the major excavations of 1987-92 at Birdoswald directed by Tony Wilmott, who contributes the main paper on this period. Wisely, perhaps, he prefers not to use a well-known autobiography that might conceivably be the work of a Briton growing up near Birdoswald at just this period. St. Patrick's *Confessio* tells us that his grandfather was a Christian priest, his father a deacon and *decurio* (of Carlisle ?), whose small country house was near a place whose name is sometimes interpreted as *Banna* near *Bernia*: Birdoswald (Jones & Mattingly 1990, 315-6; Thomas 1981, 307-314). Patrick's tantalising story at least implies that, in the post-Roman North, Christianity, urban government, and the Latin language were well established, though they faced sea-borne barbarian ravages.

The excavation evidence from another major Roman base, Corbridge, is less helpful than that at Birdoswald for late and post-Roman times; in fact little is left from any period later than the third century (Bishop & Dore 1988,139). Of late, though, there have been exciting discoveries on the banks of the Tyne nearby, and Margaret Snape's contribution indicates how a post-Roman landscape may be reconstructed from documentary sources and recent excavation.

We are still without useful archaeological remains of any kind relating to the fifth and sixth centuries in Tynedale, and there is only one inscription. A stone dating from about AD 500 that probably reads BRIGOMAGLOS [HIC] IACET was found near Vindolanda and is now at Chesters. It suggests that late in the fifth century a Christian Celtic community continued in that area (Wall 1965, 206-8; Jackson 1982).

However thin the material evidence, early literary sources suggest that Pre-Roman and Roman tribal and military organizations evolved into frontier client states, and ultimately into the little-known Celtic kingdoms of Birneich and Rheged. It is not clear which, if either, of these dominated Tynedale, but it was more likely the latter. These developments were considered at the conference in an important contribution by Rosemary Cramp, here summarised. They have also been the subject of recent papers by Dr Kenneth Dark (Dark 1992 and 1996).

Where the Roman specialists probe forward from archaeologically firm ground, Rosemary Cramp's viewpoint is that of an Anglo-Saxon specialist looking backward into the darkness from the well-documented late seventh century. It is a relief to be able to turn to near-contemporary written sources, the firm if partisan evidence of Bede. His version of the Northumbrian past, created with supreme skill from a melange of memories and traditions, is questioned by authors like Kirby (1974, 1-8). It has to be supplemented from a variety of other sources. Archaeology and air photography have played a part, though neither is noticeably helpful in Tynedale. Hope-Taylor's important excavations at the royal palace of Yeavering in the 1950s, and the major report that he published in 1977, have done much to transform our perceptions of early Saxon settlement in the region as a whole; but many of his findings have been challenged, and may not be particularly relevant in the Tynedale context. Place-names offer some promise. The Celtic stratum hereabouts is thin, confined to physical features such as *Diveles* (Devil's Water) and Plenmeller; so we can conclude, unsurprisingly, that Anglian settlement probably replaced Celtic at an earlier stage than in Cumbria. But we do not know by what stages and processes power was transferred from British Rheged to Anglian Northumbria. Perhaps it was in the aftermath of Catraeth, about AD 600; or in the crisis of 634; or at the time of Ecgfrith, Aethelthryth and Wilfrid himself. One place-name offering evidence on the nature of early settlement may be that of Hexham itself, considered in the penultimate paper.

The focus of the Anglian kingdom was far away from Tynedale, which seems to have been regarded as a remote fringe area until the arrival of the forceful Wilfrid and his monks shook it back to the forefront of development. Just how the kingdom of Bernicia came into existence and how it evolved in the century before Wilfrid's foundation is very relevant, as is the part its rulers played in the Christianization of the North. A key episode was the one recorded pre-Wilfridian incident in Tynedale, the battle of Heavenfield in (probably) 634. That story carries implications about the nature of Aethelthryth's *regio* as a political unit, and perhaps about the site of Hexham itself as the setting for a hall or even a royal palace, as suggested by Peter Ryder (1994, 216).

1. STARTING POINTS

There remain many uncertainties, We do not know what kind of people, or how many people, lived in Tynedale when Wilfrid appeared. We cannot be sure of what race, religion or culture they were, or how their communities were organized, or what their historical background was. These issues were touched on at the conference, and there were hints of a few tentative and incomplete answers. However much light the following essays shed on this fascinating period, they cannot remove the basic uncertainties about what happened in Tynedale in the two centuries before Wilfrid.

REFERENCES

Bishop M C & Dore J N 1988 *Corbridge: Excavations of the Roman fort and town 1947-80* London, Historic Buildings & Monuments Commission for England.

Breeze D J 1982 *The Northern Frontiers of Roman Britain* London, Batsford.

Breeze D J & Dobson B 1976 *Hadrian's Wall* London, Allen Lane (Penguin).

Colgrave B ed 1927 *The Life of Bishop Wilfrid by Eddius Stephanus* Cambridge UP.

Colgrave B & Mynors R A B eds, 1969 *Bede's Ecclesiastical History of the English People* Oxford, Clarendon.

Collingwood R G & Wright R P 1965 *The Roman Inscriptions of Britain* I, Oxford.

Dark K R 1992 'A Sub-Roman re-defence of Hadrian's Wall?' in *Britannia* XXIII, 111-20.

Dark K R and Dark S P 1996 'New Archaeological and Palynological Evidence for a Sub-Roman Reoccupation of Hadrian's Wall' in *Archaeologia Aeliana* 5th series, XXIV, 57-72

Hanson W S et al 1979 'The Agricolan Supply Base at Red House, Corbridge' *Archaeologia Aeliana* 5th series, VII, 1-88

Hinds A B 1896 *Northumberland County History, Vol III, Hexhamshire Part I* Newcastle, Andrew Reid.

Jackson K H 1982 'Brigomaglos and St Briog' *Archaeologia Aeliana* 5th series X, 61-5

Jones B & Mattingly D 1990 *An Atlas of Roman Britain* Oxford, Basil Blackwell.

Kirby D P ed 1974 *Saint Wilfrid at Hexham* Newcastle, Oriel Press.

Rivet A L & Smith C 1979 *The Place-names of Roman Britain* London, Batsford.

Ryder P F 1994 'The Two Towers of Hexham' *Archaeologia Aeliana*, 5th series XXII, 185-218

Selkirk R 1995 *On the Trail of the Legions* Ipswich, Anglia Publishing.

Thomas C 1981 *Christianity in Roman Britain to AD 500* London, Batsford.

Wall J 1965 'Christian evidences in the Roman period: the Northern Counties, Part I', *Archaeologia Aeliana* 4th series XLIII, 201-226.

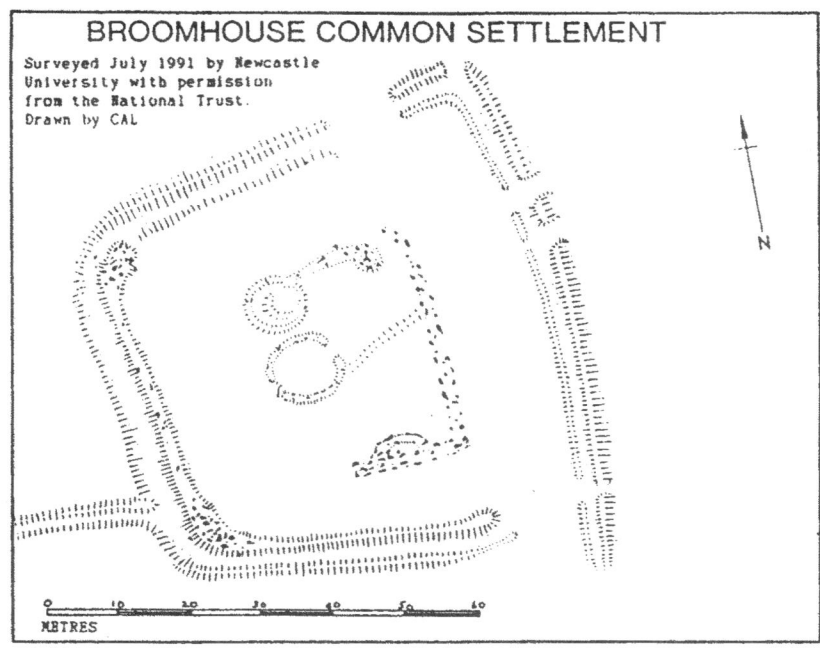

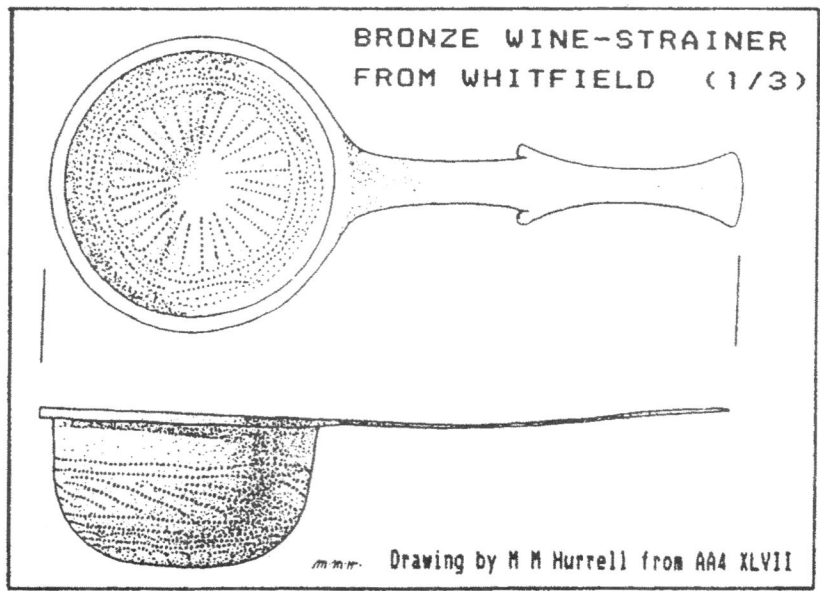

2. THE ROMANS IN TYNEDALE

Jim Crow and Tom Corfe

Roman armies campaigned in the northern counties of England from AD 71 onwards, and by the end of the decade the legions of Julius Agricola had established a campaign base at Red House, close to the river crossing at Corbridge. As the armies moved northwards into Scotland a new cross-country road was built between Corbridge and Carlisle, linking the main military highways on the west and east sides of the country. The new route across the Tyne-Solway isthmus is now called by its medieval name the Stanegate, and the easterly invasion route, Dere Street, passes through Corbridge and is followed for much of its course by the A68. Forts were built at Vindolanda and at the main site of Corbridge, and these continued to be occupied after AD 86 when the main Roman armies were withdrawn from Scotland. Whether the Stanegate and its garrisons ever constituted a formal frontier may be doubted; it was probably no more than a patrolled road like many others in the south; but in AD 122 Hadrian commanded the construction of the most substantial frontier in the Roman world from Wallsend to Bowness-on-Solway. Inevitably the study of Hadrian's Wall has dominated the region's archaeology and today Tynedale thrives on its Roman heritage. The District's official logo is a bust of Hadrian, emblazoned on road signs and council vans and the Roman occupation is proudly celebrated by the tourist and heritage industries.

Much material evidence remains from the three centuries of Roman occupation, and the most prominent memorial in Hexham Abbey is a pre-Christian one. It is a gravestone over 8ft tall found re-used as a paving slab in the slype and erected in its present position in the late nineteenth century. The monument was set up by his fellow cavalrymen to Flavinus, a young standard-bearer in the *Ala Petriana*. The famous crypt of the seventh-century church was largely built of re-used Roman stones taken from the public buildings and bridge of Roman Corbridge, and some still bear Roman inscriptions. Recent work on the contemporary crypt at Ripon has shown that it was largely built of Roman stones taken from either Aldborough or York. Clearly the temptation to recycle building materials of any earlier age was too great for Wilfrid's masons. Other

Saxon churches along the Tyne such as Corbridge and Bywell similarly incorporate many re-used Roman stones. Such later churches as Chollerton, St. Oswald's at Wall and Beltingham display Roman sculpture, columns and altars. Roman building stones appear also in such medieval buildings as the Old Gaol at Hexham and the gatehouse at Staward Peel. Names like Chesters and Chesterholm suggest the lasting impression made by surviving Roman strongholds on Anglo-Saxons, who long continued to use such Roman roads as Stanegate, Dere Street and the Military Way beside the Wall.

Strictly speaking, the arrival of the Roman armies ended pre-history, but the historical sources and inscriptions all present a Roman perspective, compiled for a metropolitan audience two thousand miles from the cold and misty northern frontier. The native population of northern Britain remains as silent

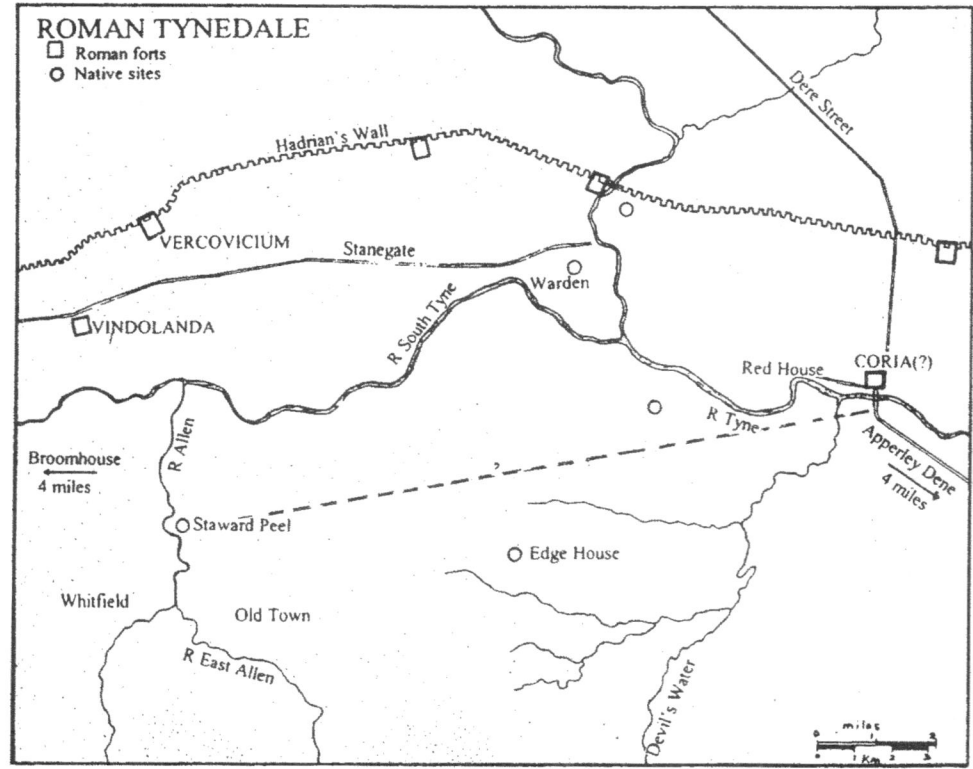

2. THE ROMANS IN TYNEDALE

and anonymous as in the preceding millennia, apart from a derogatory reference in the Vindolanda writing-tablets to the *brittunculi* or 'little brits', either native troops or the hostile local population. Tynedale formed part of the tribal confederacy known as the Brigantes, and one small grouping is recorded as the Textoverdi, located south of Vindolanda, possibly in the vicinity of Ridley Hall and the valley of the Allen, with a focus at the small hill-fort at Staward Peel. The Roman name of Corbridge, *Coria* (rather than Corstopitum), may refer to a tribal meeting place located at the route centre, which the Romans occupied. Apart from the meagre sources we must rely on the limited archaeological remains from the region for evidence of the native population.

Recently, the earliest presence of man has been pushed back several millennia with the discovery of a flint tool from near Prudhoe. This has been identified as belonging to the Late Upper Palaeolithic period; so perhaps nine thousand years before Rome (11000 BP) there were hunter-gatherers in Tynedale (Cousins & Tolan-Smith 1995). Mesolithic hunters occupied clearings in Tynedale's primeval forest, and their Neolithic farming successors carried the transformation of the Tynedale landscape a stage further (Tolan-Smith, 1996, 1997). In the second and first millennia BC a farming population occupied the valley; and on the stony ridges rising north of it many traces remain of their hut circles, homesteads and cultivated fields. Bronze axes and cist burials have been found in and near Hexham itself (Jobey 1978), most recently on the golf course. Beneath the Roman settlement at Corbridge were found the circular ditch and post-holes of an earlier settlement (Bishop & Dore 1988, 7).

This prehistoric evidence is unevenly distributed. Subsequently cultivation and urban growth have obliterated much from the Tyne valley itself. In contrast to the hills and valleys of north Northumberland, rich in the field monuments of every prehistoric period, the moorlands south of the Tyne are notably empty of archaeological evidence. This may be in part because poor land did not encourage farming, but mainly because there has been as yet little serious fieldwork in the area. The most prominent pre-Roman sites around Tynedale are on the ditched and embanked hill-tops. The Iron Age hill-fort of Warden Hill strategically overlooks the junction of the North and South Tyne Rivers, while smaller enclosed hill-top sites have left traces at Wall, on Barcombe Hill near Vindolanda (Jobey 1974, 31-2) and (a recent survey suggests) at Staward Peel. Prudhoe Castle, on its prominent hill, may conceal a similar site, and there was probably another on Windmill Hill in Hexham (Hinds 1986, 237).

Corbridge was on the direct Roman route towards Caledonia take by Agricola, and the legions chose this point to ford and later bridge the Tyne. The Red House campaign base, guarding the crossing, was succeeded within a decade by a new timber fort half a mile to the east. Like the supply base and town that followed it, this was at the junction of Dere Street, the main route from the south towards Scotland, and the Stanegate (Dore 1989). It was from this first age of conquest that the memorial to Flavinus dates. He is shown triumphantly riding down an uncouth and sinister native. Flavinus's *ala* of auxiliary cavalry apparently moved west from Tynedale before AD 98, and was eventually based at Stanwix, near the later Carlisle (Phillips 1977, no 68).

Sites like Corbridge and Vindolanda with a military connection have been very thoroughly examined, and the everyday life of the communities that developed in the associated *vici* can be studied in their excellent modern museums. Less is known of the scattered farms of Tynedale. One recent survey on Broomhouse Common, south of Haltwhistle, revealed one of the few enclosed farm sites, with a round house indistinguishable from many other farms of the pre-Roman Iron Age (see p 10). Another similar site is located near to Edge House in Hexhamshire (Jobey 1974, 32), while a further group of farmsteads and field systems is currently being studied by Robert Johnson and Josh Pollard on Hartleyburn Common south-west of Haltwhistle. Recent excavations on the line of the Haltwhistle by-pass have demonstrated for the first time an Iron Age or Roman period farmstead in the Tyne Valley, less than a mile from the survey site on Broomhouse Common (Fraser 1997). The relative rarity of native sites south of the Tyne can be attributed in part to the concentration of fieldwork in the north of the county, but also to extensive mineral extraction in the dales and moorlands of the South Tyne and Allendale, which has disturbed very large tracts of the more fertile valley sides and the uplands over the past four centuries. The few surviving settlements in this area are likely to be the relics of a more extensive settlement pattern. This is also represented by the remains of quern-stones of Roman date which are still regularly found during ploughing in the Tyne Valley and the hills around it, and decorate the gardens of many farms. Arable farming continued to be important in the Roman period, especially as there was a new demand from the garrisons on the Stanegate and on Hadrian's Wall; the quern-stones show the common use of artefacts in both military and native contexts.

Sometimes, however, other Roman artefacts did find their way into native homes. An intriguing story must lie behind a fine bronze wine-strainer found at

2. THE ROMANS IN TYNEDALE

Whitfield in 1848 and now in the Museum of Antiquities at Newcastle (see p 10). It was found with three large native cooking cauldrons, heavily used and still sooty from the fire, the whole hoard apparently making up a votive deposit. The elegant strainer, however, was of more sophisticated workmanship than the other vessels. Similar strainers have been found in Roman garrisons elsewhere in the Empire, and it was probably made in Italy. Perhaps it was brought in for use by the CO and his wife at a Tynedale fort. If so, we can speculate on just how it found its way into the possession of the Tynedale farmer who added it to his worn-out kitchenware as part of his offering. It is unlikely (though not impossible) that it reflects his own drinking habits (Smith 1969, 172-181).

In the field of religion, there is much evidence for the Roman tendency to encourage worship of local deities by merging them with their own gods; there are many altars dedicated to Mars-Cocidius or Apollo-Maponus (two of them in Hexham Abbey). Local deities worshipped in Romanised settings along the Tyne include Veteris, Mogons, Antenociticus, Silvanus and Coventina. Other relics in Tynedale of Celtic religion, untouched by Rome, include stone heads; though two found in a Hexham garden in 1971 and somewhat sensationally reported were in fact modern fakes (Ross,1973).

One native settlement that has been thoroughly examined is at Apperley Dene, beside Dere Street near Stocksfield. This was originally identified as a 'Roman fortlet' guarding the major highway, largely because of its rectangular enclosing ditch. In the 1950s and 60s George Jobey drew attention to the many native farm sites of Northumberland with just such rectangular ditches, and when Kevin Greene re-examined Apperley Dene in 1974-5 he established that the 'fortlet' was in fact such a site. The rectilinear farmstead, with a double ditch, a timber gateway, and at least one round wooden hut, was built in the middle of the second century; at this time the Roman army had moved northward from Tynedale to occupy the line of the Antonine Wall in Scotland. The farm's occupants made much use of Roman-style pottery and glassware; four fragments of glass vessels and two beads were found, parts of two or three fine samian pots, and a great deal of the coarse grey and black burnished ware common through Roman Britain. Well before the end of the century the farm had been abandoned, perhaps because Dere Street and its surroundings had become militarily sensitive once more; the Romans had withdrawn from the Scottish frontier, remilitarising Tynedale and re-occupying the nearby fort at Ebchester. Over a century later the enclosure at Apperley Dene was re-occupied for about fifty years during the fourth century. New buildings, apparently of undressed stone, were put up. This later settlement may then have had a defensive role as well as operating once more as a farm; it seems rather like the Border farms of later centuries with their towers and bastles (Greene, 1978).

There is no comparable excavation of a native site in the area immediately north of the Wall, so it is not clear how far Roman influence extended. Some of the sites excavated by Jobey and others revealed fragments of Roman pottery, and even glassware; but on the whole these sites suggest fewer links with Roman culture than observed at Apperley. It is not yet clear how much life differed for those Britons living north of the Wall from that for those who were firmly under Roman administration and in regular contact with the Roman army.

At Hexham itself, the long-running debate as to whether there was a Roman presence has hardly advanced over the last century, since the evidence was summarised in the third volume of the *Northumberland County History* (Hinds 1896, 237-240). The conclusions reached then may be considered still valid. A considerable number of inscribed Roman stones have turned up at various times in and near the Abbey. Local excavations almost invariably encounter re-used Roman stones. But no quantity of Roman pottery fragments has ever been found, such as is present at almost every Roman site, however remote and disturbed. In general the Hexham material gives an impression of an incoherent and random assemblage of bits and pieces, brought in for re-use. The 'cartload' of stones recovered from the river bed in 1887 suggests an accident with some building materials on their way from Corbridge. No Roman presence on the site of Hexham is signalled, though that is not to say that evidence of native occupation may not some day be found. It is important to recognize that the variety and quality of the inscriptions and sculptural fragments from Hexham are representative of a high status, cosmopolitan site like Corbridge rather than an ordinary auxiliary fort such as Chesters.

One Tynedale site where a Roman presence does seem likely, however, is at or near Staward Peel. There, a Roman altar was found, built into the gateway of the medieval tower; there are many other Roman dressed stones around. The altar had been dedicated by the prefect of a Gaulish cohort based at Vindolanda, four miles away. The stone may have been brought over the hilly and difficult route by later builders, but is more probably from a shrine on an undiscovered site much closer to Staward (Birley 1950). This may link with the small British enclosed site suspected at Staward. Perhaps this continued into the Roman period as a shrine and sanctuary, a religious focus loosely dependent upon the major centre at Vindolanda, and attracting the devotions of some from its Gaulish garrison. It is one aspect of the links between the Tynedale farmers, preserving much of their pre-Roman way of life and worship, and the Roman forces overseeing Tynedale from a few major bases.

Finally, it is worth noting that when Wilfrid made such conspicuous use of Roman inscribed and sculptured stones in building his new monastery at Hexham, he may have thought of them otherwise than as a readily available resource. Roman materials and Roman images were reminders of the great imperial past of Tynedale and of all Christendom, a past that Wilfrid was dedicated to reviving in a new form.

REFERENCES

Birley E 1950 'A Roman Altar from Staward Pele and Roman remains in Allendale' *Archaeologia Aeliana*, 4th series, XXVIII, 132-51.

Bishop M C & Dore J N 1988 *Corbridge: Excavations of the Roman fort and town, 1947-80* Historic Buildings & Monuments Commission for England, Archaeological Report no 8.

Cousins S & Tolan-Smith C 1995 'An Upper Palaeolithic Flint Tool from the Tyne Valley, Northumberland', *Archaeologia Aeliana* 5th series, XXIII, 307-9.

Dore J N 1989 *Corbridge Roman Site*, English Heritage guidebook.

Fraser R 1996-7 'Discoveries along the A69 Haltwhistle Bypass' in Hardie C & Rushton S *Archaeology in Northumberland 1996-1997*, Northumberland County Council.

Jobey G 1974 *A Field-Guide to Prehistoric Northumberland, Part 2* Newcastle Frank Graham.

Jobey G 1978 'A Beaker burial from Altonside, Haydon Bridge, Northumberland' *Archaeologia Aeliana* 5th series VI, 173-4.

Hinds A B 1896 *Northumberland County History*, vol III, Newcastle, Andrew Reid.

Smith D J 1969 'The Forgotten Whitfield Hoard of Bronze Vessels' *Archaeologia Aeliana* 4th series, XLVII, 172-181.

Tolan-Smith C 1996 'The Mesolithic-Neolithic Transition in the Lower Tyne Valley: a Landscape Approach', in *Neolithic Studies in No-Man's Land*, ed Frodsham P, Northern Archaeology Group.

Tolan-Smith C 1997 *Landscape Archaeology in Tynedale*, Department of Archaeology, University of Newcastle.

3. ROMAN ROADS AND BRIDGES IN TYNEDALE

Paul Bidwell

Introduction

This paper takes the form of a series of connected notes on the Roman roads and bridges of Tynedale. It does not attempt a general survey of the roads, its purpose being rather to draw attention to recent field work and publications which throw fresh light on the development and history of the system.

In an area which remained under close military control throughout the Roman period, the network of communications was entirely dominated by the needs of the army. One of these needs - supply - is illustrated in detail by the *Vindolanda* writing tablets. One of the lengthiest texts (Bowman & Thomas 1994, no 343) is a letter from a certain Octavius written at a date between 13 January and 1 March in a year which fell between AD 104 and 120. He was trying to disentangle a series of business transactions which had run into difficulties. He promised to pay his correspondent Candidus at the fort of *Vindolanda* for a hundred pounds of sinew, at the same time requesting at least part payment for 35 tonnes of unthreshed grain. Candidus had previously told Octavius that hides were ready for collection at Catterick, but Octavius wrote that he had not yet fetched them because 'I did not care to injure the animals while the roads are bad'. This is a clear statement of what previously it has only been possible to presume: that in northern Britain large quantities of material were transported by road over considerable distances. Several other documents refer to carts: one, for example, records the dispatch of 38 cart axles (Bowman & Thomas 1994, no 307).

The other principal functions of the road system were the movement of troops and the transmission of information. The *Vindolanda* tablets include no clear references to the first of these functions, but the wide range of their contents emphasises the extent to which the army relied on written records and communications. Couriers must have been seen frequently on the Roman roads in Tynedale. Other incidental uses of the roads evident or implied from the contents of the *Vindolanda* tablets included travel for social purposes: a soldier going on leave to *Coria* (probably Corbridge, Bowman & Thomas 1994, no 175) and, most famously, the attendance of Sulpicia Lepidina, wife of the prefect Flavius Cerialis, at the birthday party of Claudia Severa (no 291).

River Transport: the Piercebridge Formula

Two books by Mr Raymond Selkirk, *The Piercebridge Formula* (1983) and *On the Trail of the Legions*, (1985) have sought to show that the rivers of north-east England were subjected to large-scale engineering so that they could be used for barges supplying the Roman army. This radical theory means that for the purposes of supply the road network would have been very much of secondary importance. It has generated much discussion and a number of articles in journals of record reviewing the evidence, all taking a sceptical view. Lewis (1984), while accepting the possible importance of river transport, rejected most of the instances of Roman engineering adduced by Selkirk. Hay (1992) showed that from an engineering point of view the Roman bridge at Piercebridge, the prototype for Selkirk's theory, could not have served as a dam with locks; the forthcoming report on the bridge by Fitzpatrick should remove any doubts on this point. The most thorough review of the Piercebridge formula is by Anderson (1992), who examined Selkirk's proposed Roman lock and dam sites and rejected each one. Lewis (1995) has criticised Anderson's more general discussion of the practicalities of land and river transport; Lewis remains sympathetic to the notion that river transport enabled by engineering might have been widespread 'on the gentler gradients of the more lowland rivers', but admits that tangible proofs are lacking.

Little more can be usefully said on this subject until fieldwork produces the remains of Roman quays, dams or locks; these, as Lewis (1995, 420) has pointed out, are as likely to be of timber as of stone. Until this happens it is safer to assume that inland water transport was confined to stretches of river navigable without engineering. In Tynedale, then, it seems that military transport needs were served entirely by the road system.

Roads and the Roman conquest of northern England

The origins of the road network are rooted in the physical and political geography of the region. The effect of the former on the Roman occupation has never been better described than by Haverfield in 1907 (Haverfield ed Macdonald 1924, 99):

3. ROMAN ROADS AND BRIDGES IN TYNEDALE

[The isthmus of which Tynedale forms part] is the central fact of the north country of England. Here the span narrows to some seventy miles between open sea and sea; a valley runs across it and forms at present the principal link between east and west coasts; and harbours lie open, especially on its eastern side. Its narrowness, perhaps even more than its valley and its harbours, has made it always peculiarly important, alike as a line of defence and as a base for further advance to the northward.

Haverfield contrasted the difficulties of the western route into this area from the south with the eastern, which explains why Dere Street was always the most important route into northern Britain. But despite the relative ease of the eastern route, the Roman army made its first appearance in the Tyne-Solway corridor at Carlisle: a date of AD 72/3 for the construction of the Annetwell Street fort has been established by dendrochronological dating of timbers from its earliest buildings (Frere 1990, 320; for the chronology of the fort, Caruana 1992, 104). The Brigantian leader Venutius had been defeated and the territory of his tribe, comprising most of North Yorkshire, Cumbria, Durham and southern Northumberland, was soon absorbed into the Roman province of Britannia. His centre of power at Stanwick (near Scotch Corner) having been overrun by forces of the governor Q Petillius Cerialis, the way was clear for an advance from York over the Stainmore Pass and down the Eden valley to Carlisle (Birley 1953, 40-1).

It has long been thought that Dere Street was established during the governorship of Agricola (eg Haverfield ed Macdonald 1924, 114). It provided a direct link between the northern frontier and Lincoln, East Anglia, the eastern Midlands and London. As a result of excavations at the fort of Roecliffe, North Yorkshire (found during recent improvements to the A1, the modern successor of Dere Street), Bishop (1995, 5) has suggested that Dere Street was perhaps constructed after AD 85. Roecliffe, which seems to have been occupied AD 71-85, commands a crossing of the River Ure, but the Dere Street crossing is 1.5km to the east, just north of Aldborough where a late Flavian and Trajanic fort probably underlies the Roman town. Near the Roecliffe fort are the Devil's Arrows, a remarkable set of prehistoric standing stones which have been taken to mark an early river crossing. Bishop has argued that for the first decade or so of Roman occupation the Roman army made use of prehistoric trackways such as that which might have existed at Roecliffe. He cites similar evidence from Corbridge, where Dere Street crosses the River Tyne: an earlier site, the Red House 'vexillation fortress', is known to the west of the later fort on the

Corbridge site. This presumably controlled an earlier crossing, possibly of prehistoric origin as at Roecliffe.

The Stanegate

The two main north-south routes, Dere Street and the apparently earlier road over Stainmore and down the Eden valley to Carlisle, were linked by an east-west road between Corbridge and Carlisle. It is known by its medieval name, Stanegate; a part of it was also known as the Carelgate. Apart from the Red House (Corbridge) site, the earliest forts on its line seem to date from the later AD 80s. This at least is the foundation date indicated for Vindolanda (Birley 1994, 3), and Nether Denton, roughly equidistant from Carlisle and Vindolanda, was probably built at the same time. Carvoran may also date to the late 80s, but the fort at Old Church, Brampton, was built in the early second century. During the first few years of that century, following abandonment of the forts to the north, the Tyne-Solway isthmus became the effective northern frontier of Britain. The so-called 'Stanegate system', the forts along the road strengthened by the later addition of small forts at Haltwhistle Burn and Throp, has been regarded in the past as a frontier line, functionally a predecessor of Hadrian's Wall. This is doubtful, for there are no continuous ditches, palisades or closely-spaced towers to prevent movement across the Stanegate. What cannot be doubted is the importance that the Stanegate assumed as the main route linking the frontier forts.

A road from Corbridge to Whitley Castle?

The roads so far described are Roman trunk routes which remain in use today, even if the Stanegate is now a minor country road where its course has not been entirely lost, as between Corbridge and the North Tyne; Selkirk (1995, 111-119) and others have produced reasonable guesses about the course of this missing section. A subsidiary route was the Maiden Way from Carvoran to Whitley Castle and on to Kirkby Thore. Another minor route possibly ran from Corbridge to Whitley Castle. It was first noted on Warburton's map of 1716 and its existence was accepted by other antiquaries. These references were collected by Birley (1950, 148-51), who connected the road with bridge remains possibly of Roman date near the fort at Whitley Castle (rejected as Roman by Bidwell & Holbrook 1989, 113). Further possible evidence for this road's existence can be adduced. Maclauchlan and Hedley record traces of it running south-west of the Roman site of Corbridge, crossing the Devil's Water near Dilston Mill, where Selkirk has detected rock-cut post-holes in the river (1995, 123). Horsley shows the line of this road crossing the East Allen River a little to the north of Allendale Town and the West Allen south of Whitfield. The remains of Staward Peel, on the east side of the undivided Allen, three miles north of Horsley's line, probably indicate the actual crossing point. The main building there is of freshly quarried ashlar, but just to the east is a pinnacle of masonry, perhaps the angle of a gatehouse, consisting entirely of re-used Roman blocks. Attention has centred on the origin of these, Birley (1950, 138-9) arguing that the terrain was too difficult for them to have been brought from Vindolanda. The editors of *RIB* (Collingwood & Wright 1965, no 1688) nevertheless assumed that the altar found here, and by implication the other blocks, came from Vindolanda. Their very distinctive character has been overlooked: some blocks have lewis holes (for receiving crane hooks), one has a possible dowel hole and at least two have band anathyrosis (sides finished with roughly worked sunken panels surrounded by carefully worked margins, an economical way of achieving a close fit with other blocks). These techniques are collectively typical of *opus quadratum* (large rectangular blocks held together by metal or wooden clamps, tie-bars and dowels, with no use of mortar), which in northern Britain is almost exclusively associated with bridge construction (Holbrook & Bidwell 1989, 117-133).

The altar from Staward Peel was dedicated to *Iuppiter Optimus Maximus*, which puzzled Birley (1950, 141). He thought that if the re-used masonry came from an isolated shrine, a dedication to a local deity rather than to one commonly associated with official military religion might have been expected. For that reason he was inclined to give credence to a Roman site claimed at Old Town, about two miles south-east of Staward Peel. Reports of this from early antiquaries were doubted by Wallis and Hodgson, and no Roman finds or surface indications of early settlement have been found at either of the two adjacent farms called Old Town; but if there was a Roman bridge across the East Allen it might well have been controlled by a fortlet or small fort on this site.

The re-used masonry at Staward Peel thus strengthens the case for a Roman road crossing the River Allen. Examination of the river for a distance of two miles upstream and downstream of Staward Peel has detected no signs of a bridge, but field survey might well locate traces of the road *(cf* Selkirk 1995, 310-14).

A suggested road at Bywell

Selkirk (1983, 135-46; 1995, 102-4, 113-14) has carried out a great deal of work in the vicinity of Bywell. He suggests that a Roman road crossed the Tyne there by a bridge, the remaining piers of which were blown up with gunpowder in 1836. Dwarris (1886, 17), however, records a tradition that this bridge led to the medieval chapel of St Helena on the south side of the Tyne. Excavations north of the river found the gravel metalling of a road. Judgement on its date must await publication of the results of this work.

Hadrian's Wall

The building of Hadrian's Wall, which probably began in AD 122, had a radical effect on communications in Tynedale. From Halton Chesters to Great Chesters respectively north of Corbridge and Haltwhistle) the Wall followed the higher ground north of the River Tyne. In its final state under Hadrian movement across its line was possible at only a few points (perhaps just one in Tynedale), and then with the consent of the army. Behind the Wall was the Vallum, a continuous ditch flanked by nine-metre wide berms with mounds beyond them. This earthwork, an addition to the original scheme, could only be crossed by causeways (known as Vallum crossings) sited opposite the forts and presumably the gates of the Wall. The only major gateway in our area is at Portgate, where Dere Street crossed Hadrian's line. Portgate was presumably open to civilian traffic. It is also thought that civilian traffic could have used the Vallum crossings (themselves controlled by gates opposite the forts), though onward passage through the forts was scarcely likely to have been permitted; the alternative, it has been suggested, was to go along the north berm of the Vallum and them pass through one of the gaps in the northern mound opposite the milecastles. But road metalling on the north berm has only been recorded in one place; and, with one or two exceptions, no causeways have been found across the Wall ditch in front of the milecastles. Further excavation is required to see if there are traces of causeways across the Wall ditch at the milecastles which were removed during later stages of the occupation, but the evidence presently available suggests that passage through the Wall for civilians in Tynedale might only have been possible at Portgate.

In the original scheme for Hadrian's Wall, forts along the Stanegate were to have provided the soldiers to man the turrets and milecastles and to patrol the length of the barrier. An early modification to the scheme was to build new forts on the line of the Wall itself. This led to a large increase in the size of the Roman army in Tynedale, for the Stanegate forts at Vindolanda and Corbridge probably remained in occupation (Bidwell 1985, 10; Bishop & Dore 1989, 135, 140), and the new forts along the Wall were much more closely spaced than their predecessors. Communications between forts on the Wall was by way of the Stanegate; at first no major road was built to link the forts, milecastles and turrets directly. This curious omission was rectified when Hadrian's Wall was re-occupied after the abandonment of the Antonine Wall. However, there may have been from the start metalled tracks between the installations of the Wall; examples have been found at Denton, west of Newcastle (Bidwell & Watson 1996, 33-5) and at Tarraby Lane near Carlisle (Smith 1978, 23-4, fig 7). Gordon in 1726 and Horsley in 1732 also recorded a 'Lesser Military Way' on either side of the fort at Carrawburgh, running nearer to the Wall than the Stanegate, but all traces of it seem to have disappeared since the eighteenth century (Bidwell & Holbrook 1989, 153).

The Emperor Hadrian died in 138 and his successor, Antoninus Pius, soon decided to occupy southern Scotland, constructing the Antonine Wall across the isthmus between the Forth and the Clyde. Although Hadrian's Wall was now redundant, its associated road system remained in use. Corbridge continued in occupation, controlling the main route into Scotland, and Carlisle perhaps also served to control the western road into Scotland. The Stanegate continued as a link between these two important roads.

The return to Hadrian's Wall

Until recently it was generally accepted that Hadrian's Wall was briefly reoccupied in c158, almost immediately abandoned again in favour of the Antonine Wall, and then reoccupied again in the 160s, perhaps c163. This chronicle of indecision has recently been the subject of a penetrating analysis by Hodgson (1995), who has proposed a simpler and more plausible sequence of events: a withdrawal from the Antonine Wall had begun by 158 but some forts may have continued in occupation until the renovation of Hadrian's Wall was complete.

That renovation included improvements to the road system serving Hadrian's Wall. When the Roman army advanced into Scotland, the Vallum had been slighted by opening up gaps in its mounds at intervals of about 40 metres, and forming new causeways across the ditch with spoil from these gaps. Now a new road, the Military Way, was constructed behind the Wall, its course either running north of the slighted Vallum or along its levelled north mound. Its purpose was to connect directly all the components of the Wall; it ran from fort to fort and was connected by branch tracks to the milecastles and by paths to

3. ROMAN ROADS AND BRIDGES IN TYNEDALE

the turrets. The Stanegate still remained in use as the trunk route across the Tyne-Solway isthmus.

Other important improvements were made at the points where Hadrian's Wall crossed major rivers. Originally, the walk along the top of the Wall was carried across the rivers by stone foot-bridges; at Willowford, where the Wall crossed the River Irthing, towers gave access to the bridge from ground level, and this was probably also the case at the crossing of the River North Tyne at Chesters. Both foot-bridges were replaced by road bridges. At Chesters the new bridge was built on a monumental scale. It had four stone arches 10.8 metres in

Possible reconstruction of bridge two at Chesters. Painting by Frank Gardiner (Bidwell & Holbrook 1989).

diameter and an overall length of 58 metres; its carriageway, 6.2 metres in width, was lined on either side with stone parapet slabs set vertically in the top of moulded cornice blocks; and at intervals the parapets were interrupted by free-standing columns which were probably surmounted by statues set on decorated capitals, an embellishment known from other Roman bridges built on a large scale.

BEFORE WILFRID

The bridge has been described in detail in *Hadrian's Wall Bridges* (Bidwell & Holbrook 1989), but subsequent work in 1990 and 1991 has shown that two of the conclusions reached there were erroneous. First, the road approaching the bridge from either side ran south of the towers behind the abutments; the towers were not gatehouses as previously thought, but perhaps had the same function of surveillance as the regularly-spaced Wall turrets. The second erroneous conclusion concerned the date of the bridge. The excavations in 1982 and 1983 recovered no useful dating evidence from the construction levels, but material from the earliest occupation levels in the east tower seemed to suggest an early third-century date for the bridge. The assumption was that anything on the original floor of the tower was likely to have been deposited soon after the bridge was built. This was an argument *faute de mieux*. Better evidence emerged in 1991. In a triangular space between Hadrian's Wall, the west wall of the west tower, and the massive northern retaining wall of the road ramp, there was a thick layer of rubbish including much pottery and some discarded shoes. The pottery could be dated to mid-second century. It suggests that the road bridge was built not as part of the renovation of the Wall under the Emperor Septimius Severus in the early third century but as part of the reorganization that followed the abandonment of the Antonine Wall that seems to have started in 158.

This change in the date attributed to the construction of the bridge does not undermine the previously published explanation of its function (Bidwell & Holbrook 1989, 137-8). It was built not only to take the Military Way across the North Tyne but also traffic from the Stanegate, which was brought up to the bridge by means of a diversion. Thus, the local and arterial routes were brought under the direct supervision of the garrison at Chesters at this important river crossing. Furthermore, the construction of the bridge and the Military Way can now be seen to have been contemporaneous.

Survey and limited excavations of the Roman bridge across the Tyne at Corbridge were carried out in 1995. The identical construction methods appearing in the masonry of Chesters and Corbridge had already suggested that the two bridges had been built under the supervision of the same architect or engineer (Bidwell & Holbrook 1989, 105). Detailed examination of the southern abutment at Corbridge detected the remains of slots for lead tie-bars running across the width of the abutment, a further match with the construction techniques occurring at Chesters. Hitherto, nothing had been known of the superstructure of the bridge, but the 1995 excavations laid bare part of the road ramp approaching the southern abutment. Blocks tumbled from its revetment wall included a large octagonal plinth with moulded edges, probably intended to support the base of a statue, and moulded cornice blocks with sockets in their upper surfaces to take the uprights of a wooden parapet or balustrade.

Communications in the later Roman period and the end of the system

Little can be said of the later history of the system beyond citing the evidence for its continued use. The latest milestones from the Stanegate date to AD 306-7, 309-13 and 307-337 (Collingwood & Wright 1965, nos 2292, 2297, 2301-2), and from the Military Way to 305-6 (no 2311). The latest layer of the metalling of the road leading to the north end of the bridge at Corbridge sealed a coin of Constantine II (337-40) or Constantius II (337-61) (Forster 1908, 214, 291). At Chesters the latest coin recovered from above the metalling of the western road ramp was of the house of Valentinian (364-78). There is thus no reason to suspect that the road system went out of use before the end of the Roman period.

Indeed, much of the road system remains in use today. Not so the bridges, which did not long outlast the Roman period. The bridge at Chesters seems to have been partly dismantled in order to re-use the iron clamps that held its superstructure together. The builders of the seventh-century church at Hexham probably used the bridge at Corbridge as their principal source of stone (Bidwell & Holbrook 1989, 105); and blocks from the bridge were also re-used in the later Anglo-Saxon watermill on the north bank of the river (M Snape in this volume).

REFERENCES

Anderson J D 1992 *Roman Military Supply in North-East England: an analysis of and an Alternative to the Piercebridge Formula,* Brit Archaeological Rep 224, Oxford.

Bidwell P T 1985 *The Roman Fort of Vindolanda* Historic Buildings and Monuments Commission for England, Arch Report 1.

Bidwell P T & Holbrook N 1989 *Hadrian's Wall Bridges,* EH Arch Report 9, Historic Buildings and Monuments Commission for England.

Bidwell P T & Watson M 1996 'Excavations on Hadrian's Wall at Denton, Newcastle upon Tyne, 1986-89', *Archaeologia Aeliana* 5th series XXIV, 1-56.

Birley E 1950 'A Roman altar from Staward Pele and Roman remains in Allendale', *Archaeologia Aeliana* 4th series XXVIII, 132-51.

Birley E 1953 'The Brigantian problem, and the first Roman contact with Scotland' in *Roman Britain and the Roman Army: collected Papers*, 31-47, Kendal.

Birley R 1994 *The Early Wooden Forts* Vindolanda Research Reports I, Bardon Mill.

Bishop M C 1995 'A new Roman military site at Roecliffe, North Yorkshire', *Yorks Archaeological Soc Roman Antiq Sect Bulletin* 12, 3-5.

Bishop M C & Dore J N 1989 *Corbridge: Excavations of the Roman Fort and Town, 1947-80* Historic Buildings and Monuments Commission for England, Arch Rep 8.

Bowman A K & Thomas J D 1994 *The Vindolanda Writing-Tablets (Tabulae Vindolandenses II)*, London.

Caruana I D 1992 'Carlisle: excavation of a section of the annexe ditch of the first Flavian fort' *Britannia* 23, 45-109.

Collingwood R G & Wright R P 1965 *The Roman Inscriptions of Britain*, Vol I, Oxford.

Dwarris, Rev Canon 1886 'Notes on Bywell, AD 803-1884' *Archaeologia Aeliana* 2nd series, XI, 11-17.

Forster R H 1980 'Corstopitum: report of the excavations in 1907' *Archaeologia Aeliana*, 3rd series IV, 205-303.

Frere S S (ed) 1990 'Roman Britain in 1989: I Sites explored', *Britannia* 21, 303-64.

Haverfield F ed Macdonald G 1924 *The Roman Occupation of Britain, being six Ford Lectures delivered by F Haverfield now revised by George Macdonald*, Oxford.

Hay T T 1992 'Engineering aspects of Piercebridge Roman bridges' *Durham Archaeological Journal* 8, 63-70.

Hodgson N 1995 'Were there two Antonine occupations of Scotland?' *Britannia* 26, 29-49.

Lewis M J T 1984 'Roman navigation in Northern England? A review article' *Journal of the Railway and Canal Historical Society* 28, 118-24.

Lewis M J T 1995 'Roman navigation in Northern England? A second look' *Journal of the Railway and Canal Historical Society* 31, 417-22.

RIB = Collingwood & Wright 1965.

Selkirk R 1983 *The Piercebridge Formula* Patrick Stephens, repr Anglia 1995.

Selkirk R 1995 *On the trail of the Legions* Ipswich, Anglia Publishing.

Smith G H 1978 'Excavations at Tarraby Lane' *Britannia* 9, 19-57.

Acknowledgements

The recent work on the bridges at Chesters was funded by English Heritage and managed by N Holbrook, W Griffiths and the author. The work at Corbridge was funded by Northumberland County Council and English Heritage and managed by Mrs M Snape and the author.

4. THE AFTERMATH OF ROME
Tony Wilmott

This title was suggested by Tom Corfe, and I chose to keep it as it enshrines a perception which acts as a starting point for this paper; that is the idea of a Roman period with a definite end around 410 and definable changes thereafter, an idea with which, as will become apparent, I am not comfortable.

We are virtually wholly ignorant of the nature of the pre-Roman landscape, population, economy, society and political divisions in Tynedale and this equally applies to the north-west. We also have little grasp of the realities of the effect and extent of Romanisation on the populations of the area. Given all this, it is really not surprising that we are virtually totally ignorant of the situation in the fifth-century countryside. It has been suggested, probably with some justice, that the basic lifestyle of the indigenous local populations changed little from the pre-Roman to the post-Roman period. The greatest change may well have been the employment opportunities, and the opportunities for social betterment (at least up to 212), for members of the local populace in the *auxilia* of the Roman Army. Certainly by the third century at the latest the normal recruitment requirements of the *auxilia* are likely to have been met locally.

The types of sites for the Roman period which have been most explored have been the Wall system and the forts and their *vici*; limited islands of Romanisation within an unchanging rural sea, according to Jones and Walker (1983). Knowledge of even these sites in terms of morphology and sequences of development is not as extensive as might be thought, and it is still true that almost every excavation on such a site will spring a surprise. Certainly the least known aspects of the northern forts concern their later periods, when they must have evolved to meet the changing conditions of the later Roman Army. Much of the evidence comes from the late Roman sequence at Birdoswald.

What then was the late army of the frontier like? The units of frontier troops, or *limitanei*, were probably small. This contention is largely based on evidence from other provinces, where cohorts of 50-100 strong are recorded as early as the reign of Diocletian. Coh XI Chamavorum mustered 164, for instance (Tomlin 1979). In 411 the largest unit in Cyrenaica had 40 soldiers. On the frontiers of the Rhine and Danube, many forts would have been incapable of holding the second-century strengths of the units recorded there in the *Notitia*. At Eining the late fort was only one-tenth the size of its second-century predecessor (James 1984). There is little evidence from Britain, but the late fourth-century praetentura at Wallsend, for instance, was almost entirely devoid of buildings. At Birdoswald, the third-century granaries went out of use in the mid-fourth century. The southern building had its ventilated sub-floor filled in, and its floor relaid and continued in use, while the north granary collapsed and was levelled to the ground, the stone presumably being used to maintain other buildings in the fort. Clearly the garrison no longer required this amount of storage space for foodstuffs. Perhaps it was possible for a small garrison to derive sufficient supplies from the surrounding countryside, from whence they would come as part of the Roman tax regime. There is no evidence that soldiers worked land in their own interest, even in the eastern Empire until the 440s, and it would be a mistake to see the late Wall garrisons as soldier-farmers. The *limitanei* drew pay and supplies. Furthermore, by 313 soldiering was compulsorily hereditary (Tainter 1988, 144), and until 372 the sons of soldiers drew rations (Holder 1982, 102). By 400 the garrison of a fort like Birdoswald would be likely to comprise a small unit of soldiers mostly of local indigenous ancestry, and therefore sharing the outlook of the local agricultural community, by whom they would be supplied as a tax requirement. They would be third, fourth or more generation soldiers within hereditary military families. They would have been static for generations, with stable lives and local roots.

It has been often pointed out, after 409 or 410 (or whatever date one chooses for the 'end' of Roman Britain) the only difference, albeit an important one, is that the troops cease to be paid, or to be supplied as part of an official system. Martin Millett's (1990, 212-230) model for the period suggests that after an attack on the province in 408 and the failure of the military to deal with it, the provincial elite took responsibility for their own defence. Though legitimised by Honorius in 410, the situation sprang from a tax revolt by those paying for a system of defence and administration which no longer met their needs. If centralised authority was thus rejected, the army, as a branch of that authority, would cease to be supplied by it.

The archaeological evidence at Birdoswald is for continued occupation beyond the end of the fourth century, not for a break followed by a re-occupation. This

4. THE AFTERMATH OF ROME

fact is important as it demonstrates that the garrison there stayed put, and the settlement must have evolved in ways which would allow it to survive.

During the mid-fourth century, the southern granary was re-floored without the sub-floor ventilation associated with Roman granaries. At about the same time the north granary was demolished and turned over to piecemeal dumping. At some time after the deposition of a Theodosian coin of AD388-95, the south granary, which had been used as a domestic building with a large hearth at one end, collapsed. This was followed by the construction of a larger timber building on the wall lines of the north granary. This timber building was succeeded by the construction of another large and imposing timber building, which was deliberately sited to relate directly with the Roman west gate of the fort. If the granary was in use until c AD 420 the addition of a hundred years for each timber phase would suggest occupation until AD 620, while even allowing a conservative fifty years per phase suggests occupation continuing throughout the fifth and into the sixth century.

So what are the parallels for these buildings and what does the sequence represent? The only other structures which are demonstrably contemporary with those at Birdoswald are the well-known surface-built structures at Wroxeter (Barker 1985, 1990), the evidence for which is primarily the existence of prepared rubble platforms; and the timber hall at Cadbury Castle, Somerset, which similarly did not rely on ground-fast posts for support (Alcock 1995). The major building at Wroxeter, however, is similar to a Roman winged-corridor villa in plan. The simple rectangular plan of the Birdoswald building recalls that of the fifth/sixth-century hall buildings at Cadbury Castle. Patterns of fifth-century occupation which begin with re-use of Roman stone buildings, then the adaptation of semi-ruinous buildings by the addition of timber elements, and finally a confident rebuilding in timber, have been recognised at the villa of Rivenhall in Essex (Rodwell & Rodwell 1986), and the temple site of Uley, Gloucs (Woodward & Leach 1993). Surface-built timber structures of Roman date have been recorded on sites where timber survives - Ribchester for example and London - so this technique does have a Roman ancestry.

There is a widespread and characteristic tradition of timber building of the sixth to eighth centuries, which has been identified on a number of type-sites where particularly well-preserved building remains have been discovered, most notably at Cowdery's Down, Hants and Yeavering, Northumberland (James *et al* 1984). The features of these buildings include earth-fast uprights with walls of continuous wattling or planking. Important diagnostic features are the presence of external raking timbers which acted as buttresses, opposed axial doors in the long sides and the use of a simple double square planning module. In addition to Yeavering further buildings of its type have been identified within the frontier area at Sprouston, Roxburghshire, Doon Hill, Lothian, Thirlings and Milfield, Northumberland; and in the eighth-century Northumbrian settlement at Whithorn, Galloway.

This distribution effectively brackets Birdoswald to the east and west. The style is certainly later than the Birdoswald buildings, however, and is limited to those areas where Anglo-Saxon settlement had taken place. The Birdoswald buildings are emphatically not of this tradition. At Doon Hill, however, the earlier of the two substantial buildings (the second of which was of the tradition just described) was of a similar size to the final Birdoswald building (Ritchie & Breeze 1991). It was planned as an open hall with a tapering bay at either end, and is considered to have been its fifth/sixth-century British predecessor.

The most useful comparanda to the buildings at Birdoswald are thus the halls of the post-Roman British population of northern and western Britain at South Cadbury and at Doon Hill, generally interpreted as timber halls which would have been the feasting halls of royal officials, nobles or chieftains. Indeed the re-use phase of the south granary, with high quality finds dropped about a hearth at one end of a long narrow building, also recalls the social use of such buildings, with the most important people at the end nearest the fire. The whole plan of the final phase recalls a hall with its associated service buildings.

Real evidence for this period in other Roman places in Britain is difficult to come by. Wroxeter is of course the primary example. In forts and in the north there is a slowly growing body of evidence, including from South Shields, Vindolanda, Housesteads, Corbridge, Piercebridge and Binchester.

To return then to our late Roman unit. In the absence of evidence other than these buildings it is necessary to think more laterally about what they might be up to.

A prerequisite for survival and continuity would certainly be the potential of the local area to provide food. Birdoswald, like other forts on the western flank of Hadrian's Wall, lies in an area where cultivation is possible; the Irthing Valley is a very fertile area and arable cultivation has taken place in the immediate vicinity of the fort until recent years. It has already been argued that supply to forts had probably been levied compulsorily from the local population for some time. When central authority failed it is possible that such a relationship continued, but as John Casey (1992) has suggested, the old regime of official coercion might have given way to a symbiosis in which a local community supplied a residential garrison in return for the assurance of security in case of trouble.

During the early fifth century it would appear that the principal threat to the north of the diocese of Britain was from the Picts and Scots; but it is possible that attacks from these peoples were carried by sea, circumventing not only the Wall but also the emergent British kingdoms of the Scottish Lowlands, and attacking the more prosperous south. If this was the case, the Wall area may have been left in relative peace. The threat from the north might have come simply from small raids on the scale of guerrilla operations or banditry as elsewhere in the empire. However, given the generally troubled conditions of the period, the fact that a defended place was inhabited by an armed community might have been of major importance in allowing that community to survive.

Archaeological evidence from a number of fort sites (Wilmott 1997) now suggests that they actively outlasted the fourth century. In North Britain, at Malton a fifth-century date was adduced for the excavation of a large ditch through the buildings of the vicus, near the south east gate, and at Piercebridge the ditch was recut after the date of the latest coins. The basilica of the Roman fortress of York is seen as operating as a market hall or farm, supplying services such as smithing and meat distribution, while in an adjacent barrack the centurion's quarters continue as the high-status residential structure into which it had been converted in the later fourth century. Binchester is a good example of probable continuity, as butchery and blacksmithing took place within the former bathhouse, after deposition of the latest Roman material and before two episodes of stone robbing, the second of which was probably connected with the seventh-century construction of the church at Escomb. On the line of the Wall itself the evidence for continued use is sparse. At Vindolanda a refurbishment of the defences took place during the late fourth or early fifth century. This may have involved the deliberate piling of soil against the wall to prevent collapse, and probably took place when the occupants no longer had the resources to maintain the wall in a reasonable state of repair (Bidwell 1985, 46). This is redolent of evidence for late embanked fortification at Birdoswald. The well known Brigomaglos tombstone, with its lettering dating to c AD 500 is suggestive. There is a possible similar stone from Castlesteads (Collingwood &

Wright 1965, no. 2331). At Housesteads, the third phase of the north curtain wall collapsed, apparently late in the fourth century. It was then replaced by an earth rampart, the *terminus post quem* of which was provided by pottery of AD300+ from the preceding collapse. At the same site, adjacent to the north wall an apsidal structure found in 1898 may have been a late and/or sub-Roman church. The building lies close to a water tank, part of which was used as a long cist grave. The idea that this might reflect the continuance of Christianity into the sub-Roman period is intriguing (Crow 1995, 96-7). In the hinterland of Hadrian's Wall there is more extensive evidence from both South Shields and Carlisle for continuing occupation. At Shields the post holes in the gate were the culmination of a long sequence of activity for which the *terminus post quem* is a coin of 388 - 402 found in the top layer of road metalling in the revetted causeway through the outer fort ditch. A subsequent ditch was cut through this causeway, cutting off direct access. After a period of natural silting, this ditch was partly filled with rubble from the gate. The installation of the post holes followed this, and subsequently an inhumation cemetery was located outside the gate.

Evidence for early post-Roman occupation in forts of the other northern provinces is as rare as in Britain. The only possible example known to me is at Alzey on the Rhine, where timber-built long buildings succeed stone structures in phase 3 of a sequence which begins with the construction of the fort under Valentinian. The excavator interprets this as a mid-fifth century military re-occupation (Oldenstein 1986). In other provinces, such as Spain and Noricum, where no combined effort was made against invaders by populations or garrisons, it has been argued that 'with no concerted effort in time of trouble individual units would have been destroyed ... [or] faded away over a period of time' (Holder 1982, 103) An account of the *limitanei* of Noricum Ripense in 452 states that pay had ceased, troops sent to get pay had been killed by barbarians, and consequently only a few very small formations were left. The same pattern has been suggested for the British northern frontier. These attitudes rely on the *limitanei* maintaining a 'Roman' and 'military' role, with the double assumption firstly, that this would make them automatic victims of barbarian assault, and secondly, that there were 'barbarians' around who were bent on aggression. Another model for the response of such units is provided by Procopius (*Goth v.* 12.17) in which

> Roman soldiers ... stationed on the frontiers of Gaul to serve as guards gave themselves, together with their military standards, and the land which they

4. THE AFTERMATH OF ROME

had been guarding for the Romans, to the *Aborychi* and the Germans; and they handed down to their offspring all the customs of their fathers... For even at the present day they are clearly recognised as belonging to the legions to which they were assigned in ancient times, and they carry their own standards when they enter battle.... And they preserve the dress of the Romans in every particular, even as regarding their shoes.

Just from these few historical sources it is clear that there was a patchwork of responses to the crisis of the fifth century in the West, and it cannot be expected that the response of the *limitanei* in one province, or in one locality, would necessarily mirror that of another. Unlike the majority of the frontiers of north-west Europe, Hadrian's Wall was not overrun quickly, as is demonstrated by the successful existence in the north and west of Brittonic statelets which did not fall under Anglian control until the sixth century.

Throughout the north and west of post-Roman Britain, enclosed and fortified sites existed from the fifth to the eighth century. A recent list of such places (Alcock 1988) shows that they could have a varied structural and occupational style and history. There were refortified sites, and sites enclosed *de novo*; they could be walled in stone, embanked or palisaded, and were frequently sited upon hill tops, cliffs or promontories. Other natural defences such as marshland or open water were also utilised. They were secure refuges, and bases from which territory could be controlled. They might serve a residential and domestic role, and could be sited in a place chosen for its symbolic value. Fortified sites such as the re-occupied hillforts of the south west did not involve continuity of settlement. The best known sites are Cadbury Castle and Cadbury-Congresbury, both in Somerset, both of which are now fully published. The refortification, and the use of fifth-century imported pottery with which it is associated, are interpreted by the excavators as reflecting high status, and both of these fortifications are thought to be the centres of local rulers.

It is difficult to imagine a place which more adequately fits the desirable conditions for a post-Roman fortification than Birdoswald. It is a walled enclosure situated upon a cliff-girt river promontory, and as a location symbolic of the continuance of *Romanitas* its status as a former Roman fort would be hard to better. It seems likely that by the final period, which the average chronology would place in the later fifth century, there may not have been much difference in status between Birdoswald and the re-occupied hill forts of Cadbury Castle and Cadbury-Congresbury. It may be that Birdoswald was just one of a mosaic of enclosed and fortified places which acted as centres in the fifth-century British polities of the north and west. It has been suggested that the re-used granary might have functioned as a hall, in the sense in which that term is understood for Cadbury Castle. Its plan is very suggestive of one, long and narrow, with a hearth at one end around which high status objects have been found. The other buildings make most sense as the functional successors of this building. The best contemporary parallels in size and plan for the latest timber building are the timber halls which reflect the development of a heroic society with both Celtic and Roman antecedents in the fifth century and later. The deliberate repositioning of this building with relation to the west gate was done to emphasise its importance; the gate was now to be thought of as the entrance to the compound in which this building stood. It is possible to invoke in this context the 'echo' of *Romanitas* seen in the gate structure of Phase II at Cadbury Castle (Alcock 1995).

Birdoswald is distinct from other excavated defended places of this period in that it saw continuous use from the Roman period, and was probably still occupied by the descendants of the *limitanei* until the late fifth century. It has been assumed that the garrison throughout the later fourth century was of small size. When official supply failed, c 409, it has been suggested (p 30) that the remaining garrison might have continued to exact the customary tax levy for their maintenance from the local agricultural populace, in exchange for armed protection. This could, of course have been more or less coercive, and might result in the control of a tract of territory by the inhabitants of the fort. Higham (1992) notes that the communities of the Roman north quickly responded to the challenge of the fifth century by establishing a military capacity based around tribal kingdoms headed by warrior kings who drew their war bands 'from the same social groups within local tribal societies which had previously staffed the Roman *limitatenses*'. If this was the case the earliest military capability would be represented by the *limitanei* themselves; troops who shared the ethnic and cultural background of the people around, but who were the hereditary possessors of Roman military tradition. Such troops might enter into allegiance to a tribal leader or, if securely located, might themselves become a self-sustaining community based around a hereditary commander. Such a community might explain the fact recorded by Gildas (Dark 1994) that sub-Roman kings fought in formation and employed Roman tactics. As groups or individuals began to take over local power in the civilian areas of the provinces of Britain, establishing quasi-independent units, so might the local garrisons of northern forts establish *territoria* on a smaller scale, based upon the zone from which supplies had customarily been drawn. It is this latter model which is suggested for Birdoswald. The *limitanei* of *Banna* would have no problem of legitimacy; they would be (literally as well as metaphorically) the standard-bearers of residual *Romanitas*. This status might well have set them apart from other groupings, even though they may well have shared the same social structure, based around the hall of a 'head-man'. In this way forts like Birdoswald may have become local power centres with the potential to become 'part of the jigsaw that formed itself into the developing Northumbrian kingdom' (Johnson 1989).

The Birdoswald settlement may be regarded as successful only up to a point. Economically it was probably based upon the local exchange of goods and services rather than on subsistence. It appears never to have developed either an industrial capacity, or the capacity for long distance trade in such goods as imported pottery or glass like both Cadbury Castle and Cadbury-Congresbury. It seems likely that the settlement failed before the mid-sixth century, when such developments appear to be more common.

In contrast with the south, where new fortifications were built or where pre-Roman ones were re-used, the Roman north was amply supplied with defended places: the forts which continued in occupation until the fourth century and beyond. It may be here that the key to the sub-Roman period in the north should be sought; Alcock (1987, 252) opined that

> The role which the late Roman forts may have played in determining the geography of power in the Dark Ages is one of the great unexplored problems of the transition from Roman to Dark Age England, Scotland and Wales.

It may be that some indication of the answer to this problem is now emerging.

Kenneth Dark (1992) has invoked the post Roman evidence from the Wall as the basis for a thesis that the Wall system was refortified during the sub-Roman period, possibly *via* a power structure descended from the command of the *Dux Britanniarum* based in York. It is now possible to argue that the evidence from York itself cannot be held to support its survival as an administrative centre whose writ might run as far as Hadrian's Wall; while agreeing that the evidence from the Wall forts (the refurbishment of defences at Housesteads, Birdoswald, and Vindolanda, the Birdoswald hall buildings and the inscribed stones from Vindolanda and possibly Castlesteads) points to the development of high status secular occupation. The evidence which Dark uses spans the fifth and sixth centuries, a period during which local power groups must have been subject to change. It is possible that the inhabitants of sites on the Wall ceased to co-operate, or even became mutually hostile. Tainter (1988, 20) points out that after the collapse of complex administrative structures 'groups that had formerly been economic and political partners [may] now become strangers, or even threatening competitors'. It may be that different sites had greater or less success at different time, that status fluctuated, and that some sites may have failed earlier than others. The suggestion that Wall forts were occupied beyond the beginning of the fifth century does not mean that the occupation of various sites was both contemporary and of similar status at the same time.

The fifth century has been referred to as a lost century in the north (Faull 1984). Whatever this century in the former Roman frontier zone was like, it was different both from the Romanised fourth century from which it developed, and from the Germanic-influenced sixth-seventh centuries into which it evolved, but it seems that at Birdoswald and other sites we are beginning to see a possible model for this evolution.

REFERENCES

Alcock L 1987 *Economy, Society and Warfare Among the Britons and Saxons,* Cardiff.

Alcock L 1988 'The activities of potentates in Celtic Britain, AD 500-800; a positivist approach' in *Power and Politics in Early Medieval Britain and Ireland* (eds Driscoll S T & Mieke M R) Edinburgh, 22-39.

Alcock L 1995 *Cadbury Castle, Somerset; the early medieval archaeology,* Cardiff.

Barker P 1985 'Aspects of the topography of Wroxeter, *Viroconium Cornoviorum*' in *Roman Urban Topography in Britain and the Western Empire* (eds Grew F and Hobley B) CBA Res Rep, 59, London.

Barker P (ed) 1990 *From Roman Viroconium to Medieval Wroxeter: Recent work on the Roman City of Wroxeter,* Worcester.

Bidwell P 1985 *The Roman Fort of Vindolanda,* Historic Buildings and Monuments Commission for England, Archaeological Report No. 1.

Casey P J 1992 'The End of Garrisons on Hadrian's Wall: An Historico-Environmental Model' *Inst Archeol Bull,* 29, 69-80.

4. THE AFTERMATH OF ROME

Crow J 1995 *English Heritage Book of Housesteads* London, Batsford.

Dark K R 1992 'A Sub-Roman Re-Defence of Hadrian's Wall' *Britannia*, 23, 111-120.

Dark K R 1994 *Civitas to Kingdom; British political continuity 300-800*, Leicester.

Esmonde Cleary A S 1989 *The Ending of Roman Britain* London, Batsford.

Faull M L 1984 'Settlement and Society in North East England in the fifth century' in *Settlement and Society in the Roman North* (eds R F J Jones, P R Wilson and D M Evans) Bradford, 49-56

Higham N 1992 *Rome Britain and the Anglo-Saxons* London, Seaby.

Holder P A 1982 *The Roman Army in Britain* London, Batsford.

Isaac B 1988 ' The meaning of the terms *limes* and *limitanei*', *J Roman Studies*, 78, 125-147.

James S 1984 'Britain and the late Roman Army' in *Military and Civilian in Roman Britain* (eds T F C Bagg and A King) BAR, 136, 161-87, Oxford.

James S, Marshall A and Millett M 1984 'An Early Medieval Building Tradition' *Archaeol J*, 141, 182-215.

Johnson S 1989 *Hadrian's Wall* London, Batsford.

Jones G B D & Walker J 1983 'Either Side of Solway. Towards a minimalist view of Romano-British agricultural settlement in the North West' in Chapman JC and Mytum H C eds *Settlement in North Britain 1000 BC - AD 1000*, BAR, 118, Oxford.

Millett M 1990 *The Romanisation of Britain* Cambridge.

Oldenstein J 1986 Neue Forschungen im spatromischen Kastell von Alzey Vorbericht uber die Ausgrabungen 1981-85' *Bericht der Romisch-Germanischen Kommission*, 67, 289-356.

Procopius *Wars*, trans Dewing HB, 1914-29, Loeb, Oxford.

Ritchie A and Breeze D J 1990 *Invaders of Scotland* Edinburgh.

Rodwell W J and K A 1985 *Rivenhall: investigations of a villa, church and village 1950-1974*, CBA Res Rep, 55, Chelmsford Archaeol Trust Rep, 4, London.

Tainter J A 1988 *The Collapse of Complex Societies*, Cambridge.

Tomlin R S O 1979 'Meanwhile, in North Italy and Cyrenaica....' in *The End of Roman Britain* (ed Casey J) BAR, 71, Oxford, 253-70.

Wilmott T 1997 *Birdoswald: Excavations on a Roman Fort and its successor settlements, 1987-92*, English Heritage Archaeol Reps, 14, London.

Woodward A and Leach P 1993 *The Uley Shrines* HBMCE Archaeological Report No 17, London.

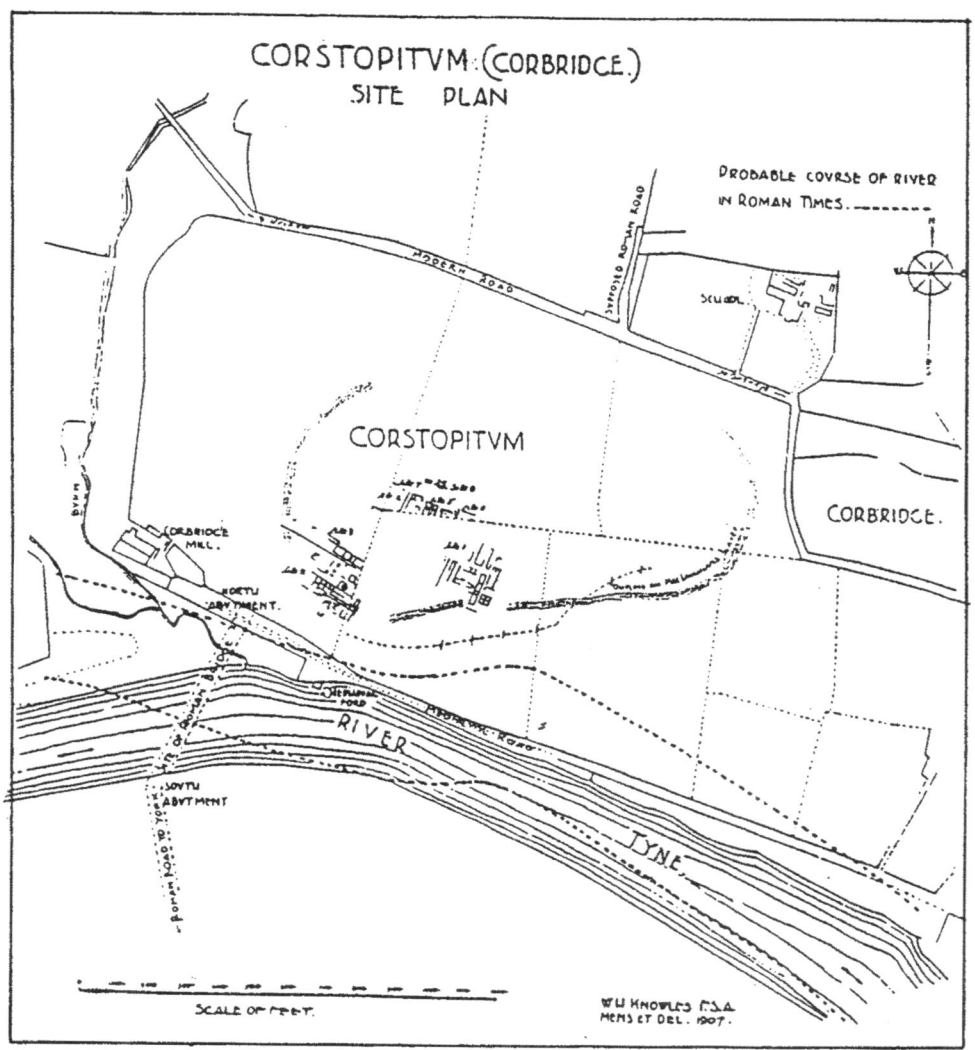

5.1. Results of the 1907 survey of Roman Corbridge. The remains of the Anglo-Saxon watermill were interpreted as part of a medieval ford. Note the modern course of the river, its presumed course in Roman times, the position of the Roman bridge, the later Corbridge Mill and the streams feeding into the Tyne. From Forster 1908, facing 216.

5. AN ANGLO-SAXON WATERMILL AT CORBRIDGE

Margaret Snape

INTRODUCTION

It has long been known that there is a platform composed of large stone blocks and timbers lying in shallow water beside the north bank of the river Tyne at Corbridge, a little downstream from the remains of the Roman bridge; however, this has been a complex and difficult structure to interpret.

It was first described by the local historian Forster in the late nineteenth century (Forster 1881, 13). Then in the early years of this century, during a large-scale survey of the Roman remains at Corbridge, the platform was studied (Woolley 1907, 180; Forster 1908, 216) and shown on plan by W H Knowles (see figure 5.1), although it was interpreted by them as a medieval quay or jetty for a medieval ford. It was surveyed by John Gillam in 1949; his unpublished plan shows that the structure had eroded since originally described. Further details are shown on unpublished photographs taken by J Jackson in the 1960s.

Two recent studies have added information on the date of the structure. In 1984 a further survey was conducted, and detailed study of the blocks showed that they were re-used Roman stones, most probably derived from the superstructure of the bridge (Bidwell & Holbrook 1989, 106-7). The structure could therefore be dated to the very end of the Roman period or later. In 1991 samples cut from two timbers were submitted for radio-carbon dating (Anderson 1992, 40-1). These placed the structure into the Anglo-Saxon period, but produced broad date ranges, centred on the ninth and tenth centuries respectively. However further observation of the structure in recent years had highlighted the continuing process of erosion.

In September 1995 an evaluation consisting of survey and limited excavation was carried out on this structure and on the southern abutment of the Roman bridge. The evaluation by Tyne and Wear Museums Archaeology Department was funded jointly by Northumberland County Council and English Heritage.

The aims of the work were to assess the precise nature of the archaeological remains and the extent of damage caused to them by erosion.

The evaluation succeeded in identifying the stone and timber structure on the northern bank as the remains of an Anglo-Saxon horizontal-wheel watermill. Secondly, in assessing the extent of erosion damage, the work revealed the instability of this stretch of the river and the great changes of course it has undergone in the past.

LOCATION, TOPOGRAPHY AND BACKGROUND

The study area is immediately to the south-west of the Corbridge Roman site (figure 5.1), which lies in Corchester Fields (also sometimes called Colchester) at the top of an escarpment. The modern village of Corbridge, about one kilometre to the east, was founded in the Anglo-Saxon period. Figure 5.1 shows the modern road, Corchester Lane, running west from the village and making two right-angled turns as it skirts the northern part of Corchester Fields. To the south, along the river bank, is a footpath which follows the line of the medieval road known as Carelgate. Also within the study area there are three streams which flow into the River Tyne. The Cor Burn flows down from the north, and the Red House Burn from the west; the streams join before turning eastwards to flow into the river (5.1 and 5.2). On the south side of the river the Devil's Water flows north from Hexhamshire to join the Tyne only a little upstream from the confluence with the Cor Burn and Red House Burn (5.3, 5.4, 5.6).

Figures 5.1 and 5.2 also show the line of the Roman bridge, the remains of its southern abutment now submerged. The bridge carried the Roman road known as Dere Street, which approached from the south-east. The line of the bridge is marked by the remains of six stone piers on the river bed, but the position of the northern abutment is unknown.

If is likely that the bridge was originally constructed to cross the river at right angles, indicating a change of course since Roman times. In Forster's survey the course of the river in Roman times was postulated (5.1), the suggestion being that it ran to the north of the present course, and also that there has been a considerable change of angle. In figure 5.1 the dashed lines representing the course of the river in Roman times run from north-west to south-east through the study area, the northern bank being aligned roughly with the modern course of the Red House Burn and with the line of the medieval Carelgate, or road to Carlisle. This position can be imagined when referring to figure 5.2.

5. AN ANGLO-SAXON WATERMILL AT CORBRIDGE

The settlement in Corchester Fields was apparently abandoned after the Roman occupation, and the focus of settlement moved to the east in the Anglo-Saxon period. The earliest reference to the modern village of Corbridge is of AD 786 (Craster 1914, 14), by which time St. Andrew's church was in existence. Presumably it was the collapse of the Roman bridge which caused a settlement shift to the present site, where the river could be more easily crossed.

Figure 5.2 shows that downstream from the point where the line of the bridge meets the northern bank is a relatively level shelf of boulders and gravel, covered by shallow water extending out from the bank for 12-20 metres before dropping steeply into the main river channel. The shelf ends c.90 metres east of the line of the bridge before dropping into a deeper pool. On it is a spread of stones, mainly boulders but with a few dressed blocks derived from the Roman bridge. The spread extends for the full length of the shelf.

The remains identified as the watermill occupy an area 18 metres by 7 metres at the eastern end of the shelf, and are covered by shallow water. They consist of a platform of large dressed blocks derived from the Roman bridge, together with large timbers. This submerged spread of stones can be seen on figure 5.2. Some indications of the early course of the river can be deduced from the position of the watermill, not parallel with the present waterline but angled north-west/south-east, roughly at right angles to the line of the bridge (5.2). However, the watermill as constructed must have stood on dry land. This suggests that during the Anglo-Saxon period the river still flowed on the same alignment as that suggested for Roman times, though its course had moved a little to the south. It is likely therefore that the edge of the submerged shelf of gravel and boulders represents the waterline in Anglo-Saxon times, either at the edge of the northern bank or the edge of an island within the river. In either case the watermill must have been standing on low ground close to the water.

The instability of this part of the river regime since the Anglo-Saxon period has resulted in great changes. Localised flooding of the northern bank has presumably washed away much of this former shelf, greatly lowering the ground level, destroying the watermill and leaving its remains submerged. To the west of the remains of the Roman bridge the change in course appears to have been even more dramatic, as described later.

THE IMPORTANCE OF THE REMAINS OF THE WATERMILL

The only other well-preserved example of this type of structure in England is a mill of mid-ninth century date at Tamworth, Staffordshire (Rahtz & Meeson

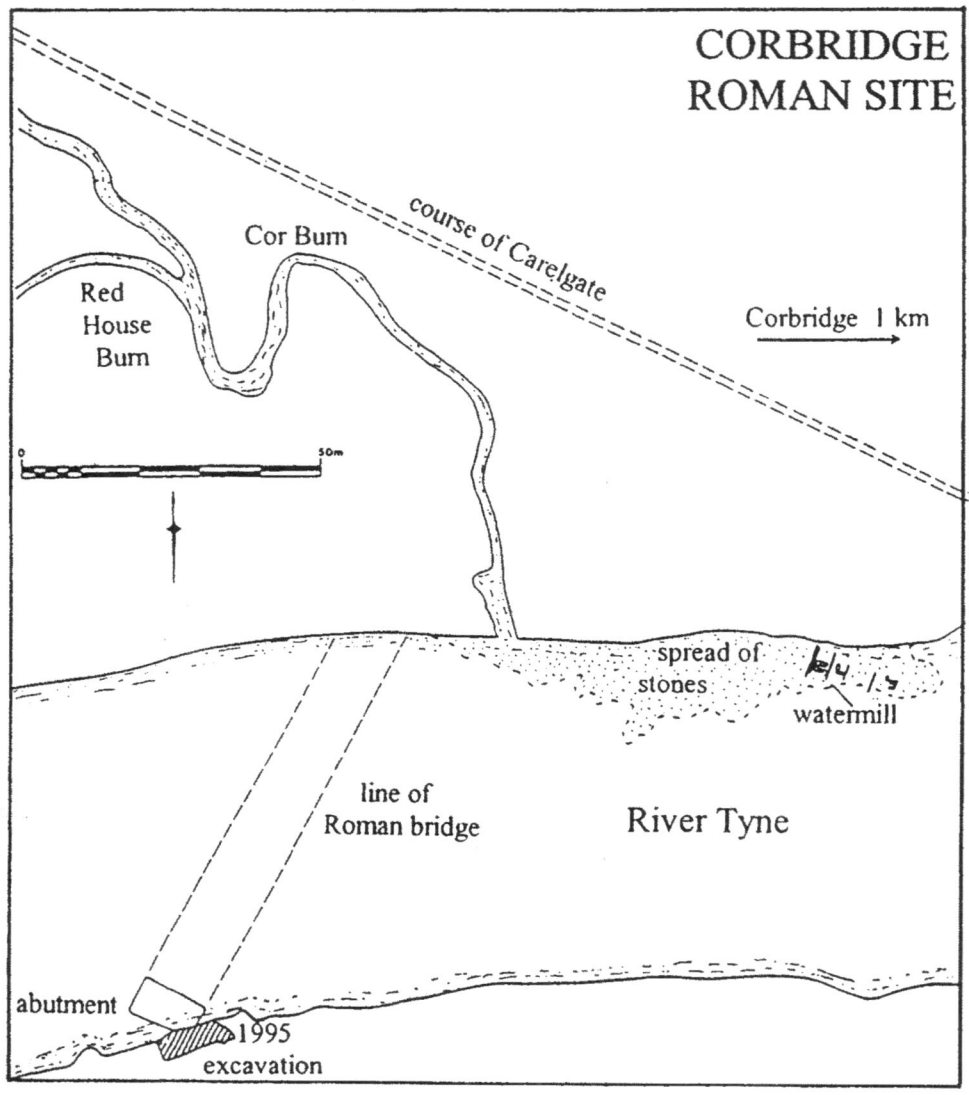

5.2. Plan based on part of a survey by Tyne and Wear Museums in 1995, showing the position of the watermill in relation to the Roman bridge, the Cor Burn, the Red House Burn, and the footpath on the line of the Carelgate.

1992, figures 31, 93, 94), though this was built entirely of timber; a few other more fragmentary examples of similar date are known, also constructed of timber. The Corbridge watermill is notable therefore not only for its state of preservation, but for the exceptional standard of its construction and the way it has been so solidly built from massive components. This becomes even more important when one realises that the handful of other examples of this type and date are all found on royal or religious sites. This obviously has great relevance for the status of Corbridge in the early Anglo-Saxon period.

Another notable aspect of the Corbridge mill is the total extent and complexity of the remains. It was clear from the outset that the remains may represent more than one wheelhouse or more than one phase, and the exact interpretation of its construction and the way in which it functioned will only become clear on further analysis. Indeed, it is not possible to give even a brief indication of how it may have worked without first discussing two other topics, the landscape in which the mill was set and a general description of the working of the horizontal-wheel type of watermill.

The limited scope of the project did not allow for detailed landscape study. However, study of cartographic and documentary sources has enabled a little to be inferred about the Anglo-Saxon landscape. This evidence is best presented by considering first the more recent maps, then moving back in time and trying to trace the earlier courses of the river in particular.

CHANGES IN THE LANDSCAPE

Nineteenth century

Although erosion of both river banks in the study area seems to have been taking place in the last two or three decades, the period from the late 1820s to the 1960s was apparently one of stability. This can be seen by comparing the modern Ordnance Survey map with the first edition, which was surveyed in the 1850s or 1860s. A map made by Greenwood in 1828, though not so accurately to scale, shows very much the same picture.

The 1908 plan (figure 5.1) was based on the Ordnance Survey and shows the area during this stable period. It is around the confluence between the Cor burn and the Tyne that the greatest changes have taken place, the main river having swung gradually further south over the centuries. Of particular interest is the oval contour line between the Red House Burn and the Tyne, which may represent the traces of what was once an island in the middle of the river.

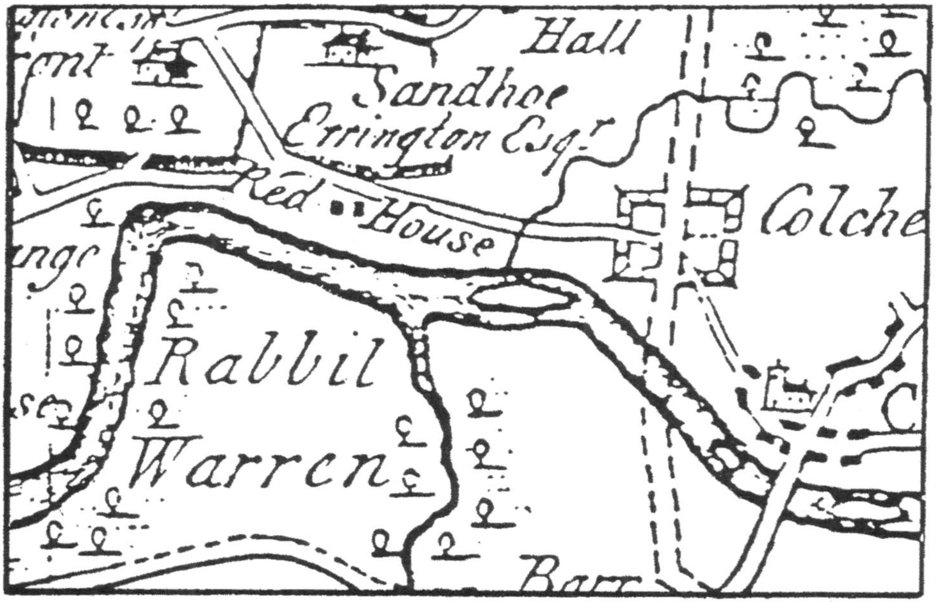

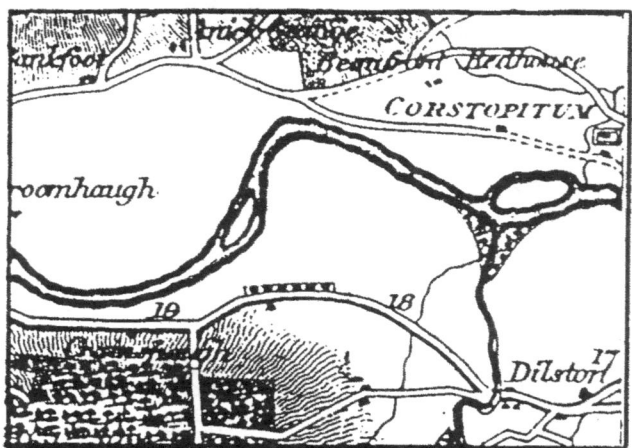

5.3. Enlarged from Armstrong's map of 1769, showing islands in the river.
5.4. Enlarged from Fryer's map of 1820, the latest map to show islands in the river in the Corbridge area.

5. AN ANGLO-SAXON WATERMILL AT CORBRIDGE

Eighteenth to early nineteenth century

A series of maps dating from 1749 to 1820 show a very different river regime from the modern one. The maps in question are:
i) a survey of 1749, carried out prior to the construction of the Military Road,
ii) Armstrong's map of 1769 (5.3)
iii) a map of Corbridge and environs by Fryer, dated 1778 (5.5)
iv) a map of Corbridge and environs by William Chapman, dated 1796
v) Fryer's map of 1820 (5.4).

What these maps have in common is that they show islands in the centre of the river. Some are beside the river crossing to Corbridge village, but more relevant to this study is the island further upstream, close to the confluence of the Cor Burn and the river. At this point the river seems wider than in the later maps, with a branch running further to the north around the island. It is known that there was a series of very big floods in 1815, 1824 and 1829, the highest being that of 1815 (Forster 1881, 45-7). This flooding was apparently sufficient to alter the river regime dramatically. Presumably the river changed its course in the vicinity of the Roman bridge, the northern branch silting up with the result that the northern bank moved southwards, incorporating the former island. Confirmation that changes in this area are comparatively recent came from a preliminary investigation of the present northern bank by Dr D Passmore of the Geography Department of Newcastle University. Analysis indicated that much of the deep silt forming the present river bank was deposited in fairly recent times.

The most useful of this series is the map drawn by Fryer in 1778 and redrawn as figure 5.5. Most field boundaries have been omitted for the sale of clarity, but those which formed the southern and western sides of Corchester fields have been included, as have those immediately to the west which form the boundaries of Bishop Rigg. Many of the present-day roads can be recognised. A road runs from the south-east to the present (seventeenth-century) bridge. To the north-west of Corbridge, Corchester Lane can be seen making its two distinctive right-angled turns around the northern edge of the Roman site in Corchester Fields. The Red House Burn can be seen at the extreme western edge of the map, running first southwards, then turning to run south-eastwards until it joins the Cor Burn and they both flow into the river. The Cor Burn, flowing down from the north, appears to have two separate streams. Actually the first edition of the Ordnance Survey map (not illustrated here) makes it clear that the westerly stream is actually the Cor Burn, while that to the east is described

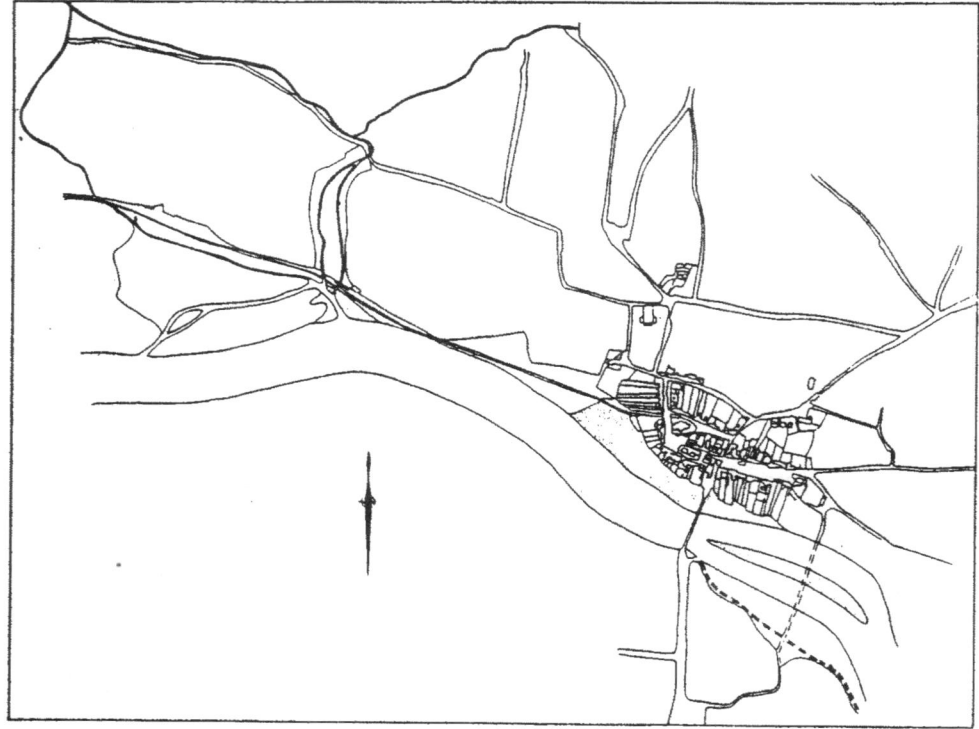

5.5. Corbridge and environs in 1778 by John Fryer. Redrawn and simplified from an original in Northumberland County Record Office (ZCL/C/1) by Ray McBride, Tyne and Wear Museums.

as an 'aqueduct' or mill race to channel water into Corbridge Mill. The rectangular building shown at the southern end of this artificial channel is the Corbridge Mill, which still survives although not as a functioning watermill. The riverside footpath of today can be recognised as a road running west from the village, first on the line of the medieval Carelgate, until it reaches Corbridge Mill. It then crosses the Cor Burn and turns north-westwards to run along the line of the Roman Stanegate, a little to the north of the Red House Burn.

However, one significant difference between this and the modern maps is the presence of an island, corresponding roughly with the position of the contour line on figure 5.1., and having a narrow channel running north of it.

5. AN ANGLO-SAXON WATERMILL AT CORBRIDGE

Middle Ages

Many features seen on the eighteenth-century maps give an indication of the landscape in the Middle Ages. The present bridge is almost on the same line as its medieval predecessor, constructed in 1236 (Craster 1914, 64-5). A plan in the *Northumberland County History* (Craster 1914, facing 136), reproduced here as figure 5.6, shows that not only was the Cor Burn important as defining the western boundary of Corchester Fields, but also that there was a strong tradition of siting watermills there, no doubt because of the force of the stream. The map shows both Corbridge Mill and a smaller building to the north, also a mill. An inset to this map, a plan of Corchester Fields in 1776 (5.7), shows an area called Miller's Close. The earliest historical reference to a mill on this stream is in 1533 (Craster 1914, 117-8), while a miller named Ralph is attested at Corbridge in the subsidy roll of 1296 (Craster 1914, 74; Fraser 1968, 47) although the site of this mill is not specified.

Figure 5.7 also shows a medieval field system surviving in the common meadows and narrow strip fields. This would explain why the medieval Carelgate only followed the Roman Stanegate to the west of the Red House Burn, and not along its line straight through the ruined Roman site; instead, it swung to the south to avoid the field system.

There is no direct evidence about the course of the river in the medieval period, but it is not unreasonable to assume that the line of the Carelgate might have run along the riverside. In that case one might imagine the island shown on 5.5 as being already in existence during the Middle Ages, with a somewhat wider channel to the north of it.

Anglo-Saxon period

What then was the landscape that the Anglo-Saxons found when they settled in this part of the Tyne Valley?

We can be sure that at least some stretches of Dere Street would have been visible to the Anglo-Saxons, the most likely perhaps being that stretch south of the Tyne, running through Broomhaugh and Riding Mill to the river crossing at Corbridge. It can be seen on 5.3 (shown as Watling Street) and the road at the south-east corner of 5.6 is on the same course.

The broad flood plain of the Tyne in this area was described by the nineteenth-century local historian Robert Forster (1881, 1-2); he cited the field names containing the word 'eales', meaning islands, as evidence of how much land

BEFORE WILFRID

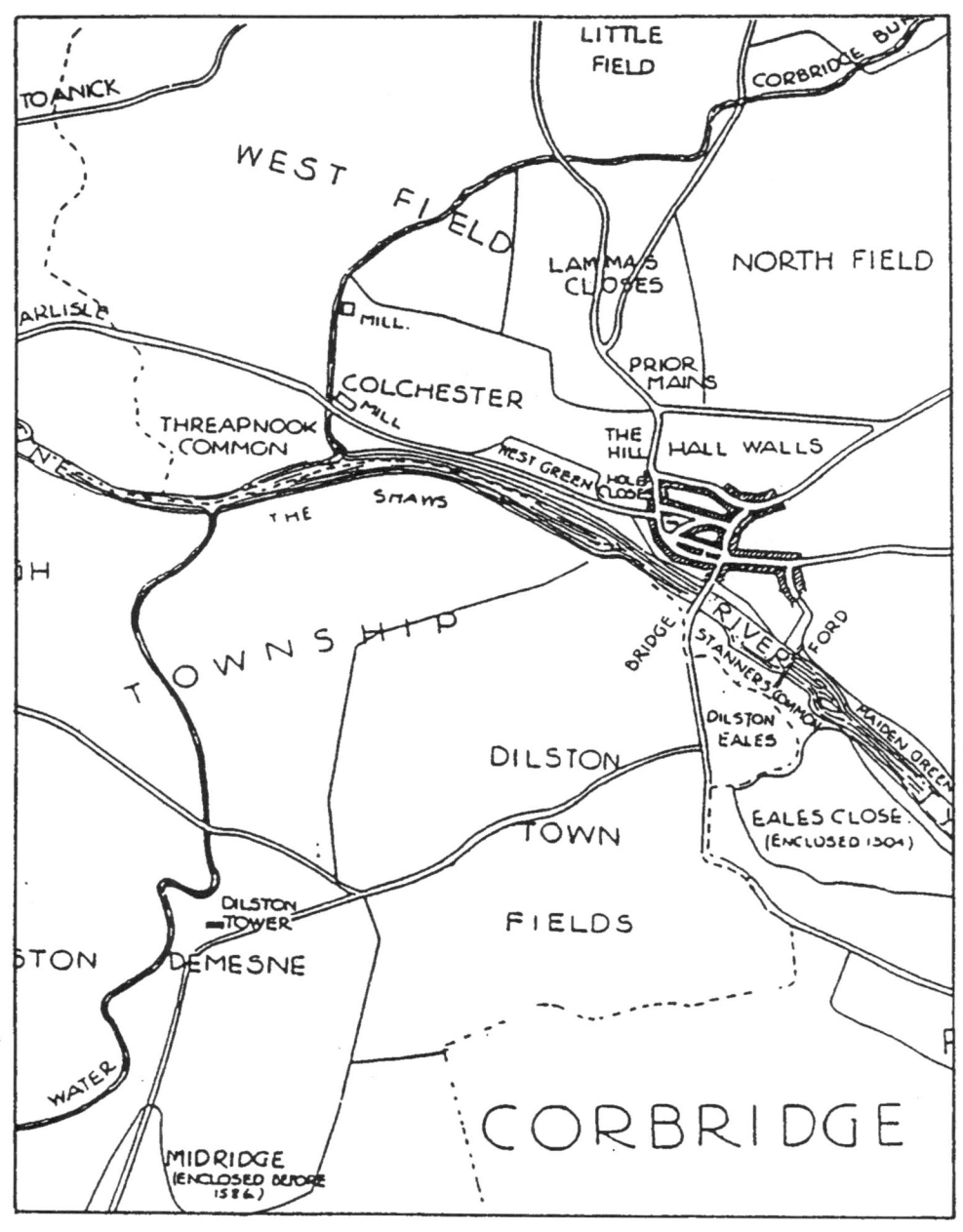

5. AN ANGLO-SAXON WATERMILL AT CORBRIDGE

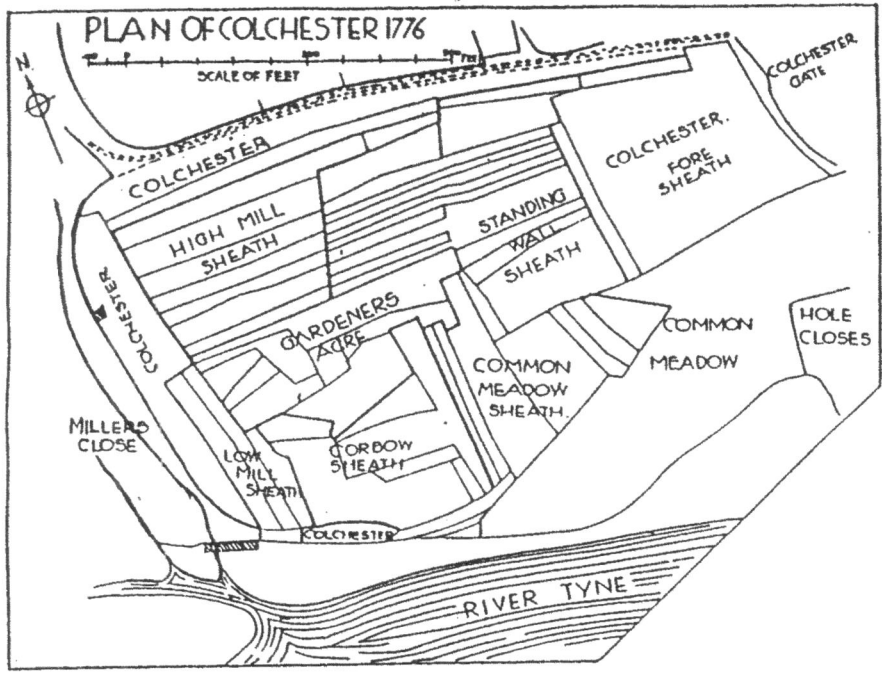

5.6. Part of a plan published in the *Northumberland County History* (Craster 1914, facing 136).

5.7. Inset to the *Northumberland County History* Plan, showing the common fields of Corbridge in 1776.

had originally been under water (Forster 1881, 4 note). Figure 5.6 shows Dilston Eales and Eales Close, the latter enclosed as early as 1304. The boundaries of these fields were evidently formed by streams, also shown on 5.5, which in addition shows a gravel bank in mid-river. We can perhaps imagine the early Anglo-Saxons negotiating a path across a broad, flat area of marsh, gravel islands, sand banks and many small shallow channels in order to ford the river. The ford shown on 5.5 and 5.6 was certainly in existence before construction was begun of the medieval bridge in 1236 (Craster 1914, 64 and plate II). St. Andrew's church, which may have been founded as early as the seventh century (Taylor & Taylor 1965, 172-6), lies only about 450 metres from the ford.

In the Roman period of course, Dere Street would have continued north-west from this point until it reached the Roman bridge. This area of flat land, now known as Dilston Haughs, may have been a marsh in Roman times. No trace of Dere Street is apparent now across Dilston Haughs, and it does not show up on air photographs. This is presumably because the road is buried under very deep layers of silt, which, like the deposits on the northern side of the river, may have formed in recent centuries (David Passmore, pers comm). We cannot know if this part of the road was still visible in Anglo-Saxon times, or whether the process of silting had already begun. In any case, even if the road were visible, it would not have been of any use to them because they could not easily have crossed the river at that point once the bridge had collapsed. The ruined bridge would have been a dramatic sight. Although the arches would have collapsed, we may imagine piers formed of huge dressed stone blocks, still standing to great height. When Wilfrid's church was constructed at Hexham in 674, it is likely that much of the stone for its construction came from the ruins of this bridge (Bidwell & Holbrook 1989, 105).

Based on the previous discussion of the river regime in this immediate area through earlier periods, one might postulate a branch of the river running further north, more along the line of the present Red House Burn, and a large island or series of small islands or gravel banks. One further fact we can surmise about the landscape in the ninth or tenth centuries is that somewhere within a reasonable distance there were mature oak trees of sufficient size to provide the massive timbers used in the watermill.

One important fact to remember is that the watermill itself would have been built on land. The watermill can be seen in figure 5.2; the area enclosed by the dashed line is now flooded, but must have been dry land in the Anglo-Saxon period. Whether it was part of an island or part of the northern river bank is unknown. We can only speculate on the complexity of streams, water channels, gravel banks and marshy ground which probably lay immediately to the north and north-west of the mill. However, we can be sure that there was a sufficient supply of water to drive the mill. The proximity of the ruined bridge as a source of stone blocks for the basement floors was another factor which made the location ideal. The source of grain might also be close to hand, if Corchester Fields were cultivated at this time; in any case, an Anglo-Saxon predecessor of the Carelgate would have provided access from elsewhere. Presumably parts of the Stanegate to the west may also have been visible.

This then was the landscape in which the watermill was built, and we can now consider how it worked.

5. AN ANGLO-SAXON WATERMILL AT CORBRIDGE

ANGLO-SAXON HORIZONTAL-WHEEL WATERMILLS

Some Anglo-Saxon watermills differed from their Roman and more modern counterparts in that the mill wheel operated horizontally rather than vertically. These are also known as 'Norse' type mills, and are also found in Scandinavia and Ireland. A detailed description of the working of Anglo-Saxon horizontal-wheel mills can be found in *An Anglo-Saxon Watermill at Tamworth* (Rahtz & Meeson 1992), from which figure 5.8 has been reproduced.

The horizontal-wheel mill was a two-storey building on land beside a river, with the mill wheel contained within a basement. Water was brought by channel or leat into a mill pool beside the building, a system of chutes or sluices

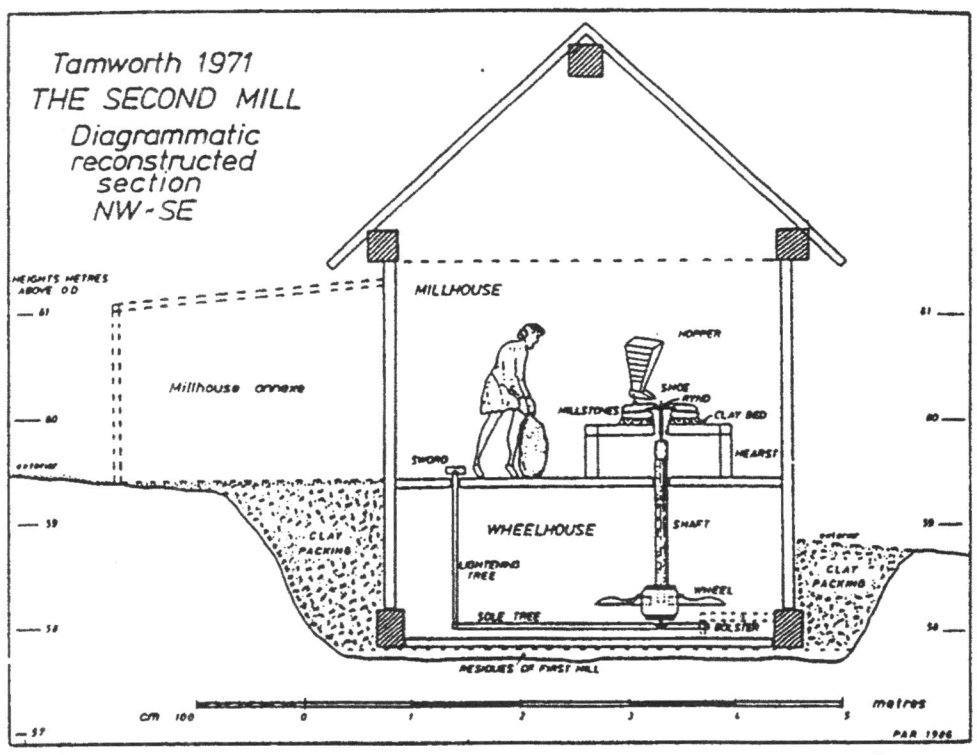

5.8. Reconstruction drawing by Philip Rahtz showing the working of the Anglo-Saxon horizontal-wheel watermill at Tamworth, Staffordshire (Rahtz & Meeson 1992, 138 figure 94).

being used to control the flow. A chute made from timber was used to direct a jet of water into the basement and turn the wheel. A shaft connected the wheel to a mill stone in an upper room, where the grain was milled; a section through the arrangement is shown in figure 5.8, though this particular section does not show the inflow or outflow of water. The floor of the basement wheelhouse had to be substantial to withstand scouring by the force of the water within it. The spent water left the basement by an outflow channel which allowed it to flow back into the river.

DESCRIPTION OF THE REMAINS AT CORBRIDGE
When the river level is high during the winter and after storms, the remains of the watermill may be submerged under several feet of fast-moving water. However, for several months during the summer the water is usually

5.9. The remains of the Anglo-Saxon watermill as seen in 1995, drawn by Graham Hodgson, Tyne and Wear Museums.

sufficiently low for the features to be clearly visible. Figure 5.9 is a sketch of the watermill as it appeared in the drought summer of 1995, when the timbers and stone blocks were partially exposed. The view from the northern bank shows the western part of the remains. Also exposed are parts of the shelf of boulders and cobbles on which the remains rest. Out in the river beyond the remains is a line of rounded cobbles, and ripples where the water is breaking over others; this is the edge of the shelf of stones and presumed to the be waterline in the Anglo-Saxon period. The watermill would have stood on dry land, the original ground surface possibly two metres higher than the present remains, which were the basement floors as seen in figure 5.8.

The western portion of the structure at Corbridge is similar in size to the wheelhouse at Tamworth. The heavy timbers at Corbridge represent sill-beams supporting a timber superstructure with a mill-room above. However, the floor of the Corbridge structure is constructed of stone rather than timber as at Tamworth. 5.9 shows two paved floors composed of large dressed blocks derived from the Roman bridge; the most westerly of these survives well, but only three blocks of the second floor remains *in situ*. The timber sill-beams vary in length from 5.3 to 6.6 metres. The carpentry of these timbers is complex and new details were recorded of the slots and mortices cut for chute emplacements or sluices and for the uprights of the superstructures. Timbers originally recorded in the eastern half of the structure are now missing, having been displaced some years ago after a storm. However, a new area of paving was discovered to the east of the known remains.

A line of stakes was seen in 1984 in the water at the north-western corner of the structure (Bidwell & Holbrook 1989, 106). Excavations in 1995 showed that this line underlay the timbers of the watermill to the east, and then continued to the west (5.9). This line is interpreted as the timber side of a millpool. However, it is not clear yet whether this pool lay mainly to the west of the mill or to the north, nor from what direction the water was channelled into the pool. It is likely that the remains of many more artificially-cut channels, leats, sluices and other structures may be preserved in the area.

CONCLUSIONS
The watermill is unique in the northern region, and only the second well-preserved example of this period in England. Such a substantial structure has important implications for the status of Corbridge in the Anglo-Saxon period. Furthermore, nothing is known of the secular aspects of settlement sites in the

North-east before the eleventh century, with the exception of princely sites such as Yeavering.

REFERENCES

Anderson J D 1992 *Roman Military Supply in North-east England*, BAR 224, Oxford.

Bidwell P T & Holbrook N 1989 *Hadrian's Wall Bridges*, Historic Buildings and Monuments Commission for England, Report 9, London.

Craster H H E 1914 *Northumberland County History*, vol 10; *Corbridge*, Newcastle, Andrew Reid.

Forster R H 1881 *History of Corbridge*, Newcastle upon Tyne.

Forster R H 1908 'Corstopitum: Report of the excavations in 1907' *Archaeologia Aeliana*, 3rd series IV, 205-303.

Fraser C M ed 1968 *The Northumberland Lay Subsidy Roll of 1296*, Society of Antiquaries of Newcastle upon Tyne.

Rahtz P A & Meeson R 1992 *An Anglo-Saxon Watermill at Tamworth*, Council for British Archaeology Research Report 83, London.

Taylor H M & Taylor J 1965 *Anglo-Saxon Architecture*, vol I, Cambridge University Press.

Woolley C L 1907 'Corstopitum: provisional report of the excavations of 1906' *Archaeologia Aeliana* 3rd series III, 162-86.

Acknowledgements

The evaluation of 1995 was carried out by Paul Bidwell and Margaret Snape of Tyne and Wear Museums. The field supervisors were Glen Foley and Jonathan McKelvey, and the survey was by Graham Stobbs. Tyne and Wear Museums are grateful to Northumberland County Council and English Heritage, who funded the evaluation; to the National Rivers Authority for their co-operation, and to Dr. David Passmore of the Geography Department, University of Newcastle, for geochemical analysis and advice. Grateful thanks are also extended to the landowners, the Hon C R Beaumont and Mr Aidan Cuthbert, for granting access to the sites, and to Messrs R Hutchinson and R Hewitt of J M Clarke and partners, agents for the Beaumont Estates, for their help and co-operation.

6. BERNICIA BEFORE WILFRID

Tom Corfe and Rosemary Cramp

This summary of Professor Cramp's lecture has been completed with her help.

Roman imperial order broke down in the northern parts of Roman Britain during the last years of the fourth century and the opening decades of the fifth. A land once divided among Latin-speaking Britons under Roman authority, free Britons, Scots and Picts, was in the course of some two hundred years transformed piecemeal into one occupied by Anglo-Saxons, Britons and Picts. At no stage can the boundaries between these fluid and overlapping groups be defined with certainty. By the early seventh century the Anglian kingdom of Bernicia had somehow emerged from the confusion in a dominant position. A major change had transformed Roman Britain into Anglo-Saxon England, disrupting old institutions and replacing the language. Debate continues as to how far that change resulted from invasion and mass migration, how far processes of acculturation and assimilation were responsible. The whole change must be seen in a wider context and longer perspective that take account of the degree of Romanization in this northern border province of the Empire.

Pre-Roman tribal territories were to some extent preserved under the Empire as units of local government; but they were also divided and re-shaped by Roman frontier works. The Wall, which dominated the North throughout the occupation, cut through existing tribal boundaries, though some at least may have reappeared in the post-Roman period. It is not clear how far Bernicia originated as a British kingdom, a development from the territories once held by the Votadini; and how far it was created by incoming Angles. Its name certainly seems to be of British topographical origin, as was that of Deira; but there must be some doubt as to whether *Bernaccia or *Berneich really was a well-defined entity, a British kingdom which Anglian rulers took over as a ready-made package.

We know very little of the Britons who lived in the region during late Roman times. They had certainly absorbed some alien traits: it is clear that in the fourth century there was a Christian stratum in native society, and that Latin was

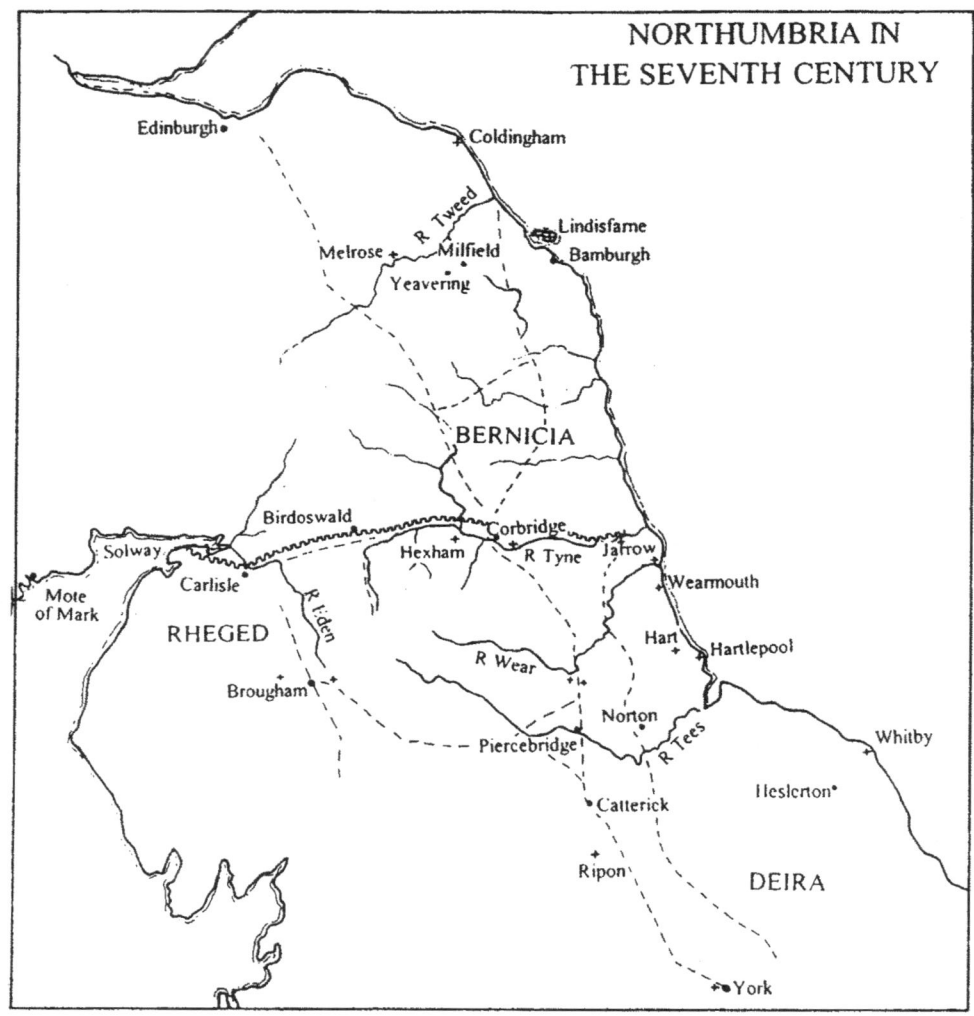

NORTHUMBRIA IN THE SEVENTH CENTURY

widely used, at least in urban circles; there are no inscriptions in the vernacular. Our understanding of how subsequent changes affected that society depends largely upon evidence from burials, house types and place names.

Burials might be expected to reflect contemporary society, but we lack extensive late Roman cemetery excavations that might give some idea of changing practice,

6. BERNICIA BEFORE WILFRID

and a full excavation of the Corbridge burial grounds would seem highly desirable. One apparent development in funerary practice within the region is the appearance of isolated cist burials within Roman structures, as at Bardon Mill, Acomb, Corbridge and Sweethope. Such cist burials (which in Scotland have been seen as post-Roman) need to be mapped throughout Northumbria, for they extend through County Durham and as far as Catterick. Crouched burials and penannular brooches, though no longer regarded as necessarily British, can be seen as indicators of continuing British traditions; such, in this area, is the Sweethope/Bavington burial, crouched with a spear in a stone coffin. Many late Roman burials contain grave goods such as coins in the mouth or lying on the body, worn and unworn ornaments (often a single bead), vessels and animal bones. Some Bernician burials, like those at Great Tosson North and Howick Heugh (Miket 1980, 293-5) apparently reflect this Roman tradition; while in the lowest levels at Monkwearmouth there were disturbed supine burials with Roman coins underlying the Anglo-Saxon monastic cemetery.

Southern Scotland has extensive cist cemeteries, while in Yorkshire there are extensive inhumation and cremation cemeteries. In Bernicia there are few of either, and the distribution seems more random. Nevertheless it is possible to detect a boundary along the line of Dere Street. Later, in the late sixth and early seventh centuries, Dere Street may have marked a boundary between Anglian settlement to the east and native rulers in the west (Cramp 1983).

One major feature of Roman Britain seems to have kept a continuing significance. Hadrian's Wall probably survived the collapse of centralised authority for a time. It certainly loomed large in the mythology of the Britons and in the writings of Gildas; it deeply impressed Bede, and was still a significant feature when such English settlements as Wall, Walbottle, Wallsend and Walwick were named. If may well have been reoccupied and reactivated under local control during the fifth century (Dark 1992), though how far it remained an effective barrier is unclear. Distribution maps of Anglo-Saxon sites such as those of Clack (Clack & Gosling 1976) suggest that the Tyne-Solway line retained importance as a frontier. Relatively dense occupation evidence survives from Northumberland north of the Wall, while in contrast a remarkably empty area appears immediately to the south of the Tyne valley. The Wall seems in fact to cast a sort of shadow, implying that what is now County Durham remained as debatable land or a buffer zone behind the frontier. The fact that a good case had been made on textual and archaeological grounds for locating the major division between seventh-century Bernicia and

Deira on the Tees rather than on the Tyne underlines the ambiguous position of this empty land between the rivers.

For a time at least the Tyne-Solway line would seem to have retained its frontier character. It must be remembered that as late as the 440s Britain retained some links with Roman authority on the continent, and with the well-organised Gaulish Church. In importing foreign mercenaries, the Britons followed good imperial practice. In such a frontier zone a screen of Germanic foederati would be a welcome addition to local forces in resisting the raids of sea-borne Picts on the east and Irish from the west. Unfortunately, in the archaeological record these troops are as invisible as the contemporary Britons; we can only distinguish those who retained distinctive native costume, and they are not to be found in Bernicia until late in the sixth century. But their influence may well have played a part in the restoration and strengthening of some existing strongpoints, whether pre-Roman hillforts or Roman forts related to the Wall. The best evidence for an intensive re-occupation of such sites comes from the Mote of Mark, just across the Solway. There is carbon-dated evidence of

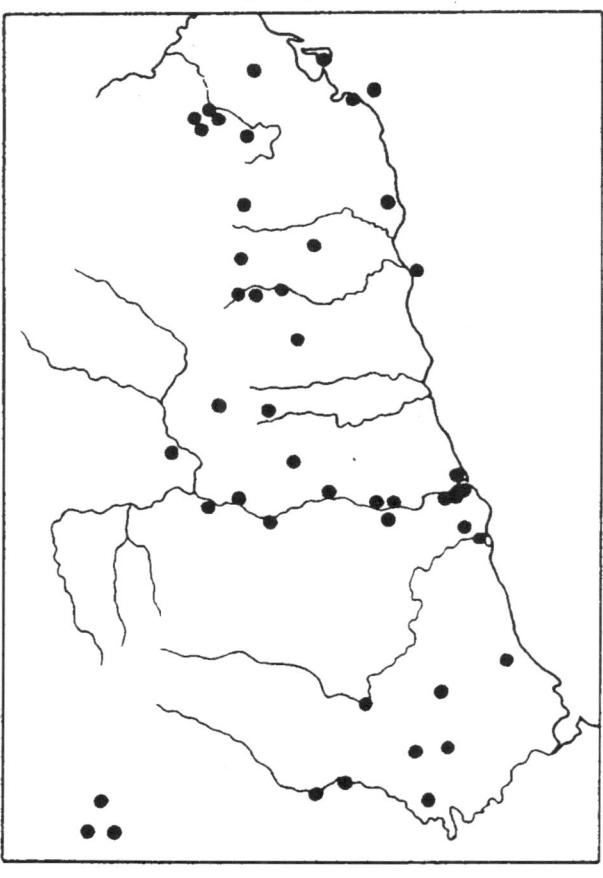

6.2. Early Anglo-Saxon sites in Northumberland and Durham, based on Clack & Gosling, eds *Archaeology in The North*, 1976.

an occupation that began in the latter half of the fifth century, continuing into the sixth and seventh (Laing, 1973). A surrounding timber-laced bank of earth and stone was constructed, while the occupants of the huts within it left many traces of their metal-working and other activities. The hill-fort at Warden, near Hexham, is another likely site for revival as a possible post-Roman defended site. Other Roman sites certainly continued in occupation. At York, once a major administrative and military centre, settlement seems to have become fragmented and polyfocal. The Roman walls were restored and rebuilt. Though the rebuilding is usually identified with an Anglian occupation, it could have taken place during any post-Roman period. In rural Yorkshire, timber farmhouse buildings and the West Heslerton Anglian cemetery suggest elements of continuity, when Roman artefacts and styles merge into post-Roman patterns; Anglian potters apparently kept up the Roman traditions. Further north, however, the evidence is less adequate. Carlisle, it has been suggested, continued into the post-Roman era as a major focus of activity and administration. It has been identified as possibly a 'capital' for Rheged, and as the major Christian centre that trained Saints Ninian and Patrick. But in fact Carlisle seems to have shrunk, and there is no firm evidence of sixth-century occupation. Local rulers are at least as likely to have operated from such places as Brougham, a major centre of activity in both prehistoric and Roman times which has clear links with Ninian as well as remains of eighth-century metalwork and an Anglo-Saxon hut. Corbridge, and indeed any other Roman civil or military settlements with evidence for post-Roman burials, might equally prove to have been centres for fifth-century activity. That Birdoswald continued to function for a time has been demonstrated archaeologically. The fifth-century evidence generally from the Tyne Valley is very slight. Much more is to be found from the following century, with the spread of violent conflict between Britons and Angles.

Arguments over the processes of acculturation or migration, and whether there was takeover by a small infiltrating elite or thorough-going conquest, are at their most extreme in the North; here, it is generally agreed, settlers of Germanic stock could only have represented a small part of the population in territories occupied essentially by Britons. In recent decades the image of ruthless foreign invaders sweeping away older ways has been discounted, and processes of adaptation and acculturation have been preferred. The arguments of C J Arnold and Nicholas Higham have gone far, in the words of Helena Hamerow, to 'demote the accounts of large-scale migrations virtually to the status of origin myths promoted by "a few thrusting chiefs" emphasising instead indigenous processes of social change' (Hamerow 1994, 166). Carrying this view to extremes, one reaches the absurd position of Britons choosing to be buried to look like Anglo-Saxons. Hamerow, though, notes that burials with distinctively Germanic dress fastenings or weapons most often appear in newly created cemeteries, though these are often quite near Roman sites. Many Anglo-Saxon cemeteries in fact attach themselves to earlier sacred sites, shrines like Uley (in the Cotswolds), Bronze Age barrows (as often in Yorkshire), tribal gathering places like Yeavering or henge monuments like Milfield. Acculturation undoubtedly took place; but it derived from a prolonged series of migrations, sometimes by large groups, sometimes perhaps by two or three families. There must have been much regional and local variation in the processes.

In Deira the presence of incoming Angles is generally more obvious at an earlier date than Bernicia. Burials show much evidence of Germanic roots; particularly through the distribution of weapon graves and of Anglian brooches. Germanic links are also apparent in the lands assumed to have been overrun by Aethelfrith. The evidence is particularly clear around Catterick, where a high-status early Anglian cemetery with distinctive sixth-century brooches suggests that the new English overlords established some sort of headquarters on a bluff overlooking the racecourse. In contrast, too few weapon graves are known in Bernicia to form a convincing picture. Whether the process was one of steady acculturation of the native population, or swift takeover by an Angle elite, the settlement of Bernicia certainly took place later than it did south of the Tees. The appearance in the sixth century of characteristic Anglian brooches does show spread of Germanic influence, and the moulds for copying Anglo-Saxon brooches found at Mote of Mark are good evidence of acculturation; Anglo-Saxon interlace on the brooches is identical with that found in Kent or Berkshire. Excavation of Yeavering and Milfield has shown adaptation and the introduction of Anglo-Saxon building techniques in a process closely paralleled all over Anglo-Saxon England. The sunken-featured huts recently identified in Cumbria and the group of wooden houses at Thirlings (O'Brien & Miket 1991), one of which has been reconstructed in replica at Bede's World, can be widely paralleled at sites as far apart as Mucking (Essex) and Heslerton (Yorkshire), for example; there is nothing distinctively Northumbrian about any of these. All that can be said is that characteristic Anglo-Saxon dress, ornament and rectangular houses, all with continental roots, gradually superseded Romano-British fashions and the round Romano-British houses throughout Bernicia.

From the mid-seventh century, the Christian centres of Bernicia became the main focal centres of cultural and technological advance. Here too the first bases in the time of Aidan were coastal, at Lindisfarne, Tynemouth and Hartlepool (demonstrating perhaps that the Pictish seaborne threat had passed). The earliest church building was in wood, though the only archaeological evidence for a wooden church from this period is at Yeavering. Mortared stone building was apparently rare before the eighth century, apart from the major monasteries inspired by Roman and Gaulish example. In other respects advance was rapid. Metallurgy, particularly the use of precious metals, flourished under monastic patronage. Literacy was imported with the Ionan missionaries, and from the late seventh century Latin inscriptions reappear in the region on name stones and on the dedication at Jarrow. At first there seems a surprising lack of literate memorials from the early Anglo-Saxon churches of the Tyne valley, except at Hexham; nevertheless, more pre-tenth century monumental inscriptions survive in the North than in southern England. Perhaps this was inspired by the wealth of Roman inscriptions in the region.

Anglian settlements seem to have occupied all the river valleys by 700. The Tyne Valley in particular was by that time a focus of Bernician Christian activity, lined with churches and on the verge of developing a rich sculptural tradition. Even then, there seems to be some sort of barrier west of Warden, the most westerly of the sequence of churches and crosses. A century earlier the continuing frontier nature of this region is much more obvious, even as it was being absorbed into the Bernician landscape. It was a frontier that faced both westward towards the Pennines and Rheged, and southward towards the no-man's land protecting Deira. The royal vill of Corbridge, beside the Dere Street frontier, guarded the major road crossing of the Tyne and remained a strategically important site. Everything west of that lay beyond the first Anglo-Saxon expansion. In this context, defended strongholds along the narrow gap of the Tyne valley might be expected to function as focal points and centres of settlement and administration.

One Tyne Valley settlement, Hexham, does indeed stand out. It alone occupies a site on the south bank of the river; every other site with Bernician links, from Warden to Bywell and Heddon, is on the north side of the valley. Hexham is set conspicuously on a defensible hill-top site, a bluff overlooking the river's flood plain at a strategically important point. The earliest name given to the place, *hagustaldes-ea*, implies an island or promontory site. It commands the empty area to the south and the hostile lands to the west, potentially the first of a chain of strong points guarding the route westward. It has much in common with such other possible early Anglian defensive sites as the promontory site of Durham or the hill top of Bamburgh. Who the Anglian (or British ?) chieftain was who first occupied the bluff at Hexham must remain uncertain, though he would seem to have been responsible for overseeing a vital and vulnerable frontier zone.

It is interesting that the grant to Wilfrid was from royal land held by the queen, presumably given her on marriage by her father-in-law. The queen's gift was Wilfrid's first landholding in Bernicia. His church at Ripon had also been endowed with lands, many of which had been recently taken from the British church west of the Pennines. It is possible that the Hexham lands could have been similarly brought under Anglian control from the British kingdom of Rheged, perhaps by intermarriage at some earlier stage. Certainly, in the later history of Hexham its missionary interest seems to have run into considerable difficulties with the see of Lindisfarne, which claimed jurisdiction in Cuthbert's day around Carlisle. The creation of a monastery and episcopal centre at Hexham introduced something of a cuckoo into the Bernician church.

REFERENCES

Clack P A G & Gosling P F, 1976 *Archaeology in the North*, Northern Archaeological Survey.

Cramp R 1983 'Anglo-Saxon Settlement' in Chapman J C & Mytum H (eds) *Settlement in North Britain 1000BC - AD1000*, BAR, Brit Series 118, Oxford, 263-97.

Cramp R 1995 *Whithorn and the Northumbrian Expansion Westwards*, 3rd Whithorn Lecture (1994), Friends of Whithorn.

Dark K R 1992 'A Sub-Roman Re-defence of Hadrian's Wall?' *Britannia* XXIII, 111-120.

Hamerow H 1994 'Migration Theory and the Migration Period', in Vyner B (ed) *Building on the Past* Royal Archaeological Institute, London, 164-77.

Harke H 1990 'Warrior Graves? The background of the Anglo-Saxon burial rite', *Past and Present* 126, 22-43.

Hope-Taylor B 1977 *Yeavering, an Anglo-British Centre of Early Northumbria*, HMSO.

Laing L 1973 'The Angles in Scotland and the Mote of Mark', *Transactions of the Dumfriesshire and Galloway Natural History and Antiquarian Society*, 3rd series 50, 39-52.

Miket R 1980 'A re-statement of evidence for Bernician Anglo-Saxon burials' in Rahtz P, Dickinson T, and Watt L (eds) *Anglo-Saxon Cemeteries*, BAR Brit Series 82, Oxford, 289-306.

O'Brien C & Miket R 1991 'The Early Medieval Settlement of Thirlings, Northumberland', *Durham Archaeological Journal*, 7, 57-91.

7. THE BATTLE OF HEAVENFIELD

Tom Corfe

The battle fought near Hexham in or about 634 marked a decisive point in the history of the North. For Bede and all who later relied on him, King Oswald's triumph over Cadwallon of Gwynedd ensured the future of Christianity in Northumbria and inaugurated a 'Golden Age'. Bede's selective view ignored both earlier mass conversions by Paulinus and the Christian credentials of the vanquished Welsh. Modern historians, more secular in outlook, regard the conflict as the decisive end for British hopes of recovering their homeland (Alcock 1971, 140-1).

In recent times the clash has been generally known as 'The Battle of Heavenfield'. That it did not in fact take place at or near the site of the cross now standing beside the B6318 has been clear since the mid-nineteenth century. Before that time is was assumed that the fight took place close by Bede's 'Heavenfield', whose precise location was also uncertain. Leland in the sixteenth Century called it 'Halydene', perhaps Hallington (Toulmin Smith 1906-10, V 61); and this confused many later writers.

The modern cross stands beside the 18th-century 'Military Road' and close to the line of Hadrian's Wall, at the crest of their rise from the Chollerford crossing of the North Tyne. Nearby, the hilltop Church of St Oswald almost certainly marks the site that Bede calls 'Hefenfeld' or 'Caelestis Campus' (Colgrave & Mynors 1969, 216-7). Eighteenth-century writers were still uncertain. Wallis in 1769 reported that '*Haly-den* i.e. the Holy Den or Vale' was best seen north of the eighteenth milestone on the military road 'watered by the *Erring-burn*, called by *Bede*, Denisburne, ... on whose banks, he assured us, the battle was fought...' (Wallis 1769, II, 112). Hutchinson in 1778 thought St Oswald's 'otherwise called Haly-den, Heauveden, or Heavenfield' was where Oswald obtained his 'singular victory' (Hutchinson 1778, 175).

Hutchinson's reconstruction set a fashion for describing the battle in imaginative detail that drew on contemporary war reporting:

> *Cedwall* advanced, arrogantly confident in his numbers, and insolent from

his victories, assuring himself of vengeance on his opposer... He attacked the intrenchments and mounted the ramparts in person; when a fatal shaft pierced his bosom, and laid him in the dust. His followers, dismayed ... halted – a panic seized them – their swords stayed from assault, and as if perplexed by inconsistent commands, they began to retire in confusion...'

Substitute a musket ball for the shaft and it could be an eyewitness report from Bunker Hill or Saratoga.

Mackenzie in 1811 unashamedly followed Hutchinson, identifying St. Oswald's as 'Haly-den, Heauveden or Heavenfield, because Oswald, King of Northumberland, obtained a singular victory over the British usurper...' (Mackenzie 1811, II 353). James Raine in 1864 marshalled supporting evidence. Arguing from Bede's statement that the Hexham brethren made annual pilgrimage in honour of St Oswald and had recently erected a church there, he noted that 'there is only one chapel or church dedicated to St Oswald in the neighbourhood of Hexham, and that is at a place about six miles from the town called St Oswalds, a little to the north of the wall, exactly in the position that Bede described, and it is just the place in which the king would choose to set up his standard' (Raine 1864, appendix ii note). St Oswald's Church has been accepted since as the site of Bede's Heavenfield. In 1927 the Revd W R Tymms, Vicar of Wall, revived the 'pilgrimage' to the site. It was he who had the modern cross set up by the roadside (Eagles 1991, 49-53).

It was James Raine (the younger), however, who identified the actual battle site some seven or eight miles due south from Heavenfield, on the Rowley Burn. This did not prevent him, and other writers since, from keeping up the tradition that Heavenfield itself was at least the starting-point of the battle, despite clear contemporary evidence that events began with an advance from the base camp at the cross. In one sense this is hardly surprising. Church and cross occupy a dominating position close to two major highways and the Roman wall, an obvious and splendid setting for one of history's most decisive conflicts. History and geography apparently lend support to the Heavenfield site. In contrast, the banks of a tiny stream in a rural backwater seem an unlikely location for so momentous a victory.

Throughout the nineteenth century the battle was usually referred to (if named at all) as Denisesburn or Rowley Burn (Sykes 1833, I, 5; Plummer 1896, II 121-3), and this usage persists among more careful writers. Sir Frank Stenton's Oxford History volume (Stenton 1943, 81) and N J Higham in *The Kingdom of*

7. THE BATTLE OF HEAVENFIELD

Northumbria, AD 350-1100 (Higham 1993, 127) use these forms. Others avoid any description more precise than 'a battle near Hexham' or 'near the Roman Wall'. But in popular tradition and often in scholarly usage Oswald's triumph remains 'The Battle of Heavenfield' (Hunter Blair 1970, 101; Stancliffe & Cambridge, 1995, *passim*).

This has led astray some respectable and responsible authors and most of their readers, as well as assorted tourists and pilgrims. It has caught out the county authorities responsible for erecting the roadside notice-board. Eagles (1991, 21 and 179 note 26) explains that in designing this the Planning and Economic Development Committee of Northumberland County Council

> encountered difficulties because of the paucity of information... Consequently they produced their own 'story' of the conflict

with the very cautious and qualified approval of Professor Richard Bailey. It is easy to fall into the trap of assuming that the Battle *of* Heavenfield took place *at* Heavenfield, and once such a misunderstanding becomes widely accepted, supporting evidence and confirmatory traditions speedily materialise. Battlefields usually come packaged with tales of mass burials or weapon finds, and Hodgson (1840, 284) provided just such evidence:

> In a field opposite Saint Oswald's chapel, called the Mould Field, and just south of the Carlisle road, I was told in 1810, that bones, skulls, and hilts of swords are frequently dug up; and tradition says, a great battle was fought here. Was this the site of part of the battle of Heavenfield, which Bede says was fought just north of the Roman Wall, and in memory of which the Chapel of St. Oswald was built?

Mackenzie in his 1825 edition used Hodgson's information, noting that 'in a field near [St. Oswald's] skulls of men and hilts of swords have been frequently ploughed up' (1825 II, 301-2). By 1860, however, a local resident was expressing doubts; in a paper read to the Newcastle Antiquaries William Coulson (Coulson 1861), a local resident, put in a question mark:

> a field close to Oswald's ... called Moulds close or the Mould close, is traditionally pointed out as the scene of the battle; sculls and swordhilts (?) having, as it is said, been ploughed up there.

This is cautious and vague. Yet now the finds in Moulds Close are regularly cited as firm evidence, not least in the roadside board, which asserts that 'A large number of skulls and sword hilts have been uncovered in a field known as Mound's [sic] Close'. Coulson's 1860 paper had been, incidentally, rather less cautious in reporting his investigation of a nearby cist burial, where 'it may be fairly assumed that these bones are the remains of Cedwalla'. The cist overlooked the Erring Burn, so Coulson (or his editor) had no hesitation in heading his paper 'The Battle of Denisesburn'.

A wide variety of convincing reconstructions of the battle have been located at the tempting Heavenfield site. This prominent hill, marking the western end of a sandstone ridge, has steep approaches on the north and west, and wide views in every direction. It is beside a major cross-country route and close to the main Roman highway to the North. Its ancient and famous fortification encouraged writers to deal with Oswald's situation in 'backs-to-the-Wall' terms. Reconstructions have inevitably been coloured by recent military experience. James Raine concocted for his documentary collection of 1864, *The Priory of*

7. THE BATTLE OF HEAVENFIELD

Hexham, (Raine 1864, xi-xiii) a splendidly dramatic version of the battle. He was writing when the Charge of the Light Brigade and Tennyson were fresh in every mind.

In 634, Oswald, who had been hiding in Scotland, left his retirement, and, eager to recover the throne that belonged to him, resolved to attack Cadwalla. It was necessary for the assailant to be extremely cautious, and on that account he drew up his forces in a position of great natural strength some seven or eight miles to the north of Hexham. Here there is a plateau of very considerable altitude, which, without any artificial appliances, presents the appearance and the advantages of a vast fortified camp. The ground on the summit is tolerably even, and must in Oswald's time have been covered entirely with heather. The place ... bore, previous to the struggle, the name of Heavenfield, an allusion no doubt to its lofty and exposed position. Oswald could not have drawn up his forces in a better place. Along the whole of the western side the platform was unassailable, for it is protected by steep banks which descend abruptly to the river of North Tyne... Towards the south also, and on a portion of the eastern side, there are hills and fells of no mean altitude. Across the upper end of this great natural fortification ran the Roman wall, but between it and the northern side of the plateau there is a space left on which a small army might be drawn up ... Oswald therefore ... took up a position at the north-west corner of the plateau, behind the wall. In that angle ... probably on the mound which the chapel now occupies, Oswald set up the famous wooden cross to be the standard of his men... To the north-west there is a long stretch of pasture land, and the eye passes on to Swinburn and Humshaugh, and far up the river in the direction of the Cumbrian hills. Over this ground it is probable that Cadwalla brought his men, and the opposing armies could see each other for miles before they closed. The troops of Cadwalla would break like a wave against the rock-bound corner in which the cross was standing, to be cast back again with little or no difficulty by its defenders. The assailants, foiled as they must have been at this point, would naturally move towards the east, where the ground is less steep and more open ... and the fight ... would go roaring eastwards.

This vivid account, with Cadwallon (a form closer to the Welsh original than Bede's 'Cadwalla') arriving from a surprising direction, bears no relation to Bede's description of the battle, despite Raine's inclusion of the *Historia Ecclesiastica* text as the opening document of his collection. Even more surprising, it was in the same volume that Raine printed evidence proving that the battle had actually taken place eight miles away.

An equally dramatic battlepiece appears in the normally sober volume IV of the *Northumberland County History* (Hodgson 1897, 177-8):

> The battle ... took place, according to Beda, at a place before then called Hefenfelth ... Oswald encamped his men on ground strongly defended by nature on one side, and shielded to the north by the Roman Wall, which (then standing) afforded a protection against Cadwalla advancing from the south, probably along Watling Street. Of the details of the battle we know nothing. How it ebbed and flowed, how the small body of men, fired with patriotic and religious ardour, withstood the assault of the larger one, flushed with previous victories and maddened with the desire for vengeance ... The spot where Oswald had camped commands a prospect over a wide and far-stretching land of hill and valley, an outlook dear to all Northumbrian hearts; an epitome, indeed, of that larger country which makes up Northumberland. To his little army it was home, with all the ties that braced their nerves and inflamed their courage to sweep away the invader and oppressor ... The battle went against Cadwalla, his army was broken, and himself flying southward from the field was slain at Denisesburne, now Rowley Water ...

It may be that in 1897, the year of imperial apogee, memories of Rorke's Drift and Khartoum still lingered in the author's mind.

Since then vigorous accounts have multiplied, thought most historians accept that the evidence is insufficient for any detailed descriptions of this fighting (Alcock 1971, 140-1). Speculative, spirited and glamorised battlepieces continue to appear. Each feeds upon its predecessors, each offers new, but equally ill-founded, variations. Thomas Hodgkin, in his 1906 volume of the *Political History of England* (Hodgkin 1906, 151-4), had Oswald place his father's veterans in ambush 'behind either wall or *vallum*'. John Sadler in 1988 (Sadler 1988, 25-9) worked out a convincing Welsh attack from the east leading to a truly epic struggle. He added an attractive drawing of Oswald's armour (modelled on Sutton Hoo), and included Cuthbert on Oswald's staff just at the time of the saint's birth. None of these versions bears any resemblance to the battle as described in its own time. Jonathan Eagles undertook elaborate fieldwork and a thorough survey of sources for a 1991 thesis, yet was unable to tear himself away from the attractions of the Heavenfield site. Surprisingly, in quoting Bede

7. THE BATTLE OF HEAVENFIELD

on the death of Cadwallon, he omitted the vital phrase 'with his whole army', which might have altered his view of the battle (Eagles 1991, 18).

There are in fact three versions of Heavenfield by near-contemporary authors who could claim some access to reliable witnesses. The first recorded account of the battle was given by the victorious King Oswald to Abbot Segene of Iona. Segene in effect headed the Scottish Church from 623/4 to 652, throughout Oswald's short reign. It was to him that the Northumbrian king appealed for missionaries to convert his people, though this story of their meeting is the only evidence that Oswald must have revisited Iona, his home while in exile, in the aftermath of his success. The story that Oswald then told was heard also by other members of the community, one of whom, Failbe, in 669 became in turn abbot of Iona. Failbe, before his own death in 679, passed on what he had heard from Oswald to his successor Adomnan, who recorded it in his Life of Columba (Anderson & Anderson 1961, 198-203).

The Iona monks who re-told and recorded this tale were more interested in Oswald's links with his Irish mentors than in sordid details of warfare. Adomnan's account makes no mention of Heavenfield, or Oswald's cross, or the site of the battle. He says simply that Oswald, sleeping on his pillow, had a vision of Columba telling him to go forth from the camp during the following night. Oswald passed on this saintly advice to his council, who represented a people 'shadowed by the darkness of heathenism and ignorance.' They were so impressed that they promised to accept baptism after the coming battle. Adomnan goes on

> On that same following night ... king Oswald advanced from the camp with a much smaller army, to battle against many thousands. And as had been promised to him, a happy and easy victory was granted to him by the Lord. King Catlon was slaughtered; and the victor, returning from the battle, was afterwards ordained by God as emperor of the whole of Britain (Anderson & Anderson 1961, 201).

Bede's account (Colgrave & Mynors 1969, 212-7), compiled some thirty years after Adomnan wrote, drew on traditions of the battle preserved by his friend Bishop Acca and the community at Hexham. The monks of Hexham naturally took a close interest in the battle fought nearby, re-telling its story and propagating the cult of St. Oswald (Thacker 1995, 107-11). The first chapter of Bede's Book III tells how

> Oswald came with an army, small in numbers but strengthened by their

faith in Christ, and destroyed the abominable leader of the Britons together with the immense force which he boasted was irresistible, at a place which is called in the English tongue, *Denisesburn*, that is the brook of the *Denise*. (Colgrave & Mynors 1969, 214-5).

This is clear and unequivocal:
infandus Brettonum dux cum inmensis illis copiis ... interemtus est in loco...

There is no suggestion of a desperate Saxon defence of a strong position. There is no question of the Welsh King being slain in flight after the battle; he and his army were destroyed together at the Denisesburn. There is no scrap of evidence for the long pursuit, so often dramatically described, of eight miles over rough country, during which the fleeing Briton must have crossed the formidable barrier of the Tyne only to be trapped, drowned or otherwise slaughtered by a stream that is rarely more than a few inches deep or a few feet wide. The only difficulty is that the name of the Denisesburn passed out of use at some time in the late Middle Ages. When Leland investigated he learned nothing of its whereabouts. In his and Camden's day the tradition was that 'Oswald won the batelle at Halydene a 2 myles est from S Oswaldes Asche. And that Haliden is it that Beda caullith Havenfeld. And men thereaboute yet finde smaule wod crossis in the grounde.' (Toulmin Smith 1906-10, V 61; Coulson 1861,/103). This led to suggestions that the fight took place at Halton, four miles east from Heavenfield, or at Hallington, five miles north-east.

The identity of the Denisesburn might have been lost, but there was indeed a stream close to the Heavenfield site; the Erring Burn. It is a little over a mile north of the ridge on which St Oswald's stands, and there is a continuous if uneven slope. It is a stream of no great size but of early importance. It may retain a name given in Celtic times, though 'Erring' is perhaps a later back-formation from Errington, recorded in 1280 (Ekwall 1960; Watts 1996); and it long marked the northern border of Hexhamshire. It was natural to identify the Erring as Bede's Denisesburn, and easy to envisage a running fight dropping directly northwards to where the burn enters the North Tyne. Sites close by at Cocklaw, Bingfield and Grindstonelaw were favoured as settings for the battle. Though the Denisesburn is now known to be much further from Heavenfield, the image persists of a compact and continuous battle somehow linking the two. Alternative versions present it as a running fight roving over a wide area, or a rambling lone flight by Cadwallon from the victors.

The present accepted identification of the Denisesburn was made in the 1860s.

7. THE BATTLE OF HEAVENFIELD

In July 1862 a party from the Tyneside Naturalists Field Club walked from Hexham to St Oswald's, Fallowfield, the Erring Burn, Cocklaw and Chollerford. Reporting on the outing in the following year (Greenwell 1864, 12-14), the Club's president, the Revd William Greenwell, noted that

> The place where this battle, which according to Beda occurred A. D. 635, was fought, has been a fertile subject of controversy. Beda tells us that is was at Denisesburn, a locality not now to be identified under that name. The field of battle was, without doubt, situated at no great distance from where Oswald erected the cross... A charter of the thirteenth century, granting lands to an Archbishop of York, seems to fix the place on the south side of the Tyne, and up the Devil's Water, that is, if we may allow the name Denisesburn to settle the point ... though we might from Beda's account have looked to find the battle field nearer to the wall, yet the name Denisesburn must be held, I think, almost conclusive on this point, for it is very unlikely that there should be in the same neighbourhood two places of that name.

Greenwell went on to quote the charter, anticipating Raine's publication of it in the following year in his *Priory of Hexham* (Raine 1964, appendix i-ii). The charter is dated 23rd November 1233. Archbishop Walter Gray granted Thomas of Whittington

> twenty acres of land from his waste in Ruleystal, between these boundaries, namely between Deniseburn and Divelis, beginning to the east upon the Divelis and rising to the great road which leads up to the forest of Lillewude.

This identifies the Denisesburn as the modern Rowley Burn, which joins the Devil's Water near Steel. It is, however, the only reference apart from Bede's to the Denisesburn, and it should be treated with some caution. Bede may possibly have known of a people called the Denise, the (English ?) group then holding the land watered by the burn. But the Latin is ambiguous, and he may be referring to 'the brook of Denisus', a name which Victor Watts suggests perhaps derives from a British form *Dubnissos*, incorporating *dubn*, the Old Celtic word for 'deep'; this would well describe the miniature gorge that the Rowley Burn forms near Steel (Watts 1996). Denise or Denisus, people or place, by the thirteenth century only the burn's name preserved any relic of Bede's time, with no hint as to that name's original significance nor of the conflict on its bank. Yet however unlikely the position seems for a major battle, and though five centuries separate the only two references to it, it remains unlikely (as Canon

Greenwell pointed out) that there were two similarly named streams so close together. If the Erring Burn's name is indeed Celtic, it will have acquired that name long before Bede's time; if the Denisesburn's name implies 'deepness', then it would seem inappropriate for the easy gradients of the Erring Burn.

Along the south side of the Rowley Burn the ground forms a low ridge, about 500 ft above sea-level and a little over a mile long. The hill on which Whitley Chapel stands marks its western end, with Steel near its eastern terminus. This tongue of land with the Rowley Burn on its northern flank and the Devil's Water to the south is rather less than half a mile wide. The two streams meet just below Steel, at Peth Foot. The whole area is overlooked by higher ground to north and south, and is best seen as a whole from around Dotland a mile to the north (over 750 ft) or Dukesfield and Slaley Forest to the south, where the ground rises to over 1000 ft.

The name of Whitley, covering a small district, suggests that this may have been a well-drained clearing in woodland during Anglian times. The present churchyard has something of the appearance of an early defensive site; but if it was one it has left no documentary or archaeological record. Near by begins the 'Broad Way', a well-defined green road across Hexhamshire Common. Of unknown antiquity, it was used once by lead-carriers and drovers and now serves hikers and sportsmen. This was presumably the 'great road' of 1233, for it heads up to Lilswood Moor and beyond it to upper Allendale. The Whitley-Steel ridge would seem to be a likely site for an encampment of the Welsh army, and here Cadwallon may have been surprised by Oswald's assault in the elusive battle.

It was only after he had given his brief account of the fight that Bede went on to describe its preliminaries. In all save one text (from early in the 8th century), a chapter division separates the story of the battle itself from the preceding events, the erection of that significant cross (Colgrave & Mynors 1969, 214-5). The Heavenfield cross mattered to Bede and to the monks of Hexham far more than the battle that followed. He tells how the monks from Wilfrid's abbey venerated the site

> where Oswald, when he was about to engage in battle, set up the sign of the holy cross and, on bended knees, prayed God to send heavenly aid...

and goes on to give a detailed account of Oswald's making and setting up to the cross, of how it was fixed in position, and of how he led a prayer meeting before the army

7. THE BATTLE OF HEAVENFIELD

advanced against the enemy just as dawn was breaking, and gained the victory their faith merited. Innumerable miracles of healing are known to have been wrought in the place where they prayed ... And even to this day many people are in the habit of cutting splinters from the wood of this holy cross...

with many resulting miracles. It should perhaps be noted that Bede's '*...et sic incipiente diliculo in hostem progressi* . . . ' leaves no doubt that it was the march that began at dawn, not the actual assault on the enemy.

Bede was intrigued by the name of this place of prayer and miracles, *Caelestis Campus*; a name which, he suggests,

it certainly received in days of old as an omen of future happenings; it signified that a heavenly sign was to be erected there, a heavenly victory won, and that heavenly miracles were to take place there continuing to this day.

This passage night seem to suggest that the 'heavenly victory' was actually won at Heavenfield, though clearly Bede's intention was to credit it to the miracle-working cross set up there. He tells how

To this place the brethren of the Hagustaldian (Hexham) Church, not far away, have long made it their custom to come every year, on the day before that on which King Oswald was killed, to keep vigil ... to sing many psalms ... to offer up the holy sacrifice ... And since that good custom has spread, a church has lately been built there so that the place has become still more sacred and worthy of honour in the eyes of all. And rightly so, for as far as we know no symbol of the Christian faith, no church, and no altar had been erected in the whole of Bernicia before that new leader of the host, inspired by his devotion to the faith, set up the standard of the holy cross when he was about to fight his most savage enemy.

Because Adomnan makes no mention of Oswald's setting up of a cross, it has been suggested (Stancliffe & Cambridge 1995, 63 note 145) that Bede's informants may have mistakenly developed their tradition around a cross erected to mark the actual site of the battle rather than its preliminaries; and there was indeed a time gap in which memories might have grown confused. In Bede's day the church had only recently been built to mark a site made famous a century earlier, and though the pilgrimage dated from the early days of Wilfrid's foundation, even that was some forty years after the battle. By that time stories may well have developed and locations may have been lost, though it is not impossible that survivors of Oswald's host were still about. Yet the Hexham tradition seems remarkably clear that the battle took place at the Denisesburn, and that the cross erected beforehand was somewhere else.

In fact, the story as told by Acca/Bede complements rather than conflicts with the Oswald/Adomnan version. Both make clear that Oswald advanced to surprise his enemy, either by night or at first light. And both celebrate Oswald's remarkable decision to fight as a Christian.

This was a bold and in some ways surprising move. It seems likely that (as Adomnan specifically says) most of Oswald's Northumbrian followers were at best only superficially Christianised. On the other hand, Oswald's opponent was unequivocally Christian, though from Bede's viewpoint his Christianity was tainted. However, there may have been a lingering Christian tradition among a British substratum of the Northumbrian people. This, the Welsh sources suggest, may have been nurtured by links with the Christian kingdom of Rheged (Chadwick 1963, 162-6). Further, Oswald may have had Christian allies from Scotland (even monks from Iona) or from Rheged itself to aid him. Oswald's elder brother Eanfrith, and his cousin Osric, had not had those allies when they sought to rescue Bernicia and Deira from the invaders by appealing for pagan support. Their tactics had proved disastrous, and fatal for both. In the wake of this failure, Oswald chose an alternative course to seek Northumbrian unity and win his neighbours' support.

Whether influenced by his vision or not, Oswald seems to have been sincere in his faith. Bede's story now links with that Adomnan. After his disturbed night Oswald first convinced his Northumbrian council, then set up his cross and delivered his pep-talk to rally the whole army. There was no undue haste about his move. He presumably know where his enemy was to be found, and expected him to stay there; it seems as though Cadwallon must have been established in a firm base. The next night Oswald mustered his men before it was light, led then south as dawn broke, and took that encampment by surprise, before his enemy was ready for action.

The one other near-contemporary source derives from Oswald's Welsh enemies. It appears in slightly different versions in the *Historia Brittonum* put together by Nennius and the *Annales Cambriae*, in the same British Library manuscript. These refer to Oswald killing Cadwallon 'in the battle of Catscaul, with a great slaughter of his army', and 'the battle of Cantscaul in which Cadwallon fell'

7. THE BATTLE OF HEAVENFIELD

(Jackson 1963, 34, 45). The identification of the battle with the Heavenfield site meant that the Welsh 'Cantscaul' was interpreted as *cad-gwal* or *cath-ys-gwaul*, 'the battle within the wall' (Greenwell 1863-4, 12 note). This has been described (by Kenneth Jackson) as absurd, and it is now generally accepted (Jackson 1963, 34, 45; Corfe 1991, 45; Watts 1995, 5) that *cant y scawl*, 'the enclosure of the young warrior', is a direct translation of *Hagustaldesham*, Hexham. The Hagustaldian monastery was known to both English-speaking Northumbrians and Welsh-speaking Britons of Rheged; and both knew that the great fight had taken place close by. The Welsh sources add nothing to the detailed geography of the battlefield, though their evidence about the northern British kingdoms, the 'Men of the North' helps to explain the background to the battle.

The position of the battlefield and the sequence of events seem clear from the contemporary evidence. But topographically and strategically the Rowley Burn remains a less obvious site for an historic encounter than the hill-top by Hadrian's Wall, so close to two main roads. Its geographical improbability must be partly responsible for the general disinclination to recognize the Whitley site as the likely scene of battle.

Oswald's force, freshly inspired and briefly rested, needed to move from its rallying-point at Heavenfield to the Rowley Burn in time to catch Cadwallon's army off guard. On the modern map it appears no easy journey. The distance, as the crow flies, is just over seven miles. The ground is uneven, dissected by streams, though none (except perhaps some stretches of the Rowley Burn itself) constituted a serious obstacle. They had to cross the Tyne. If they advanced by way of the old-established Corbridge crossing place, Oswald's warriors would have had to cover approximately ten miles. Starting at or before first light, helped by local guides and some intelligence of their enemies' whereabouts, they had to cover ground that was uneven but by no means a trackless wilderness. Whether or not there was a network of Roman roads as suggested by Raymond Selkirk, (Selkirk 1995, 102-129) the Tyne valley had many small farming settlements and was probably still dominated by the urban centre at Corbridge; well-used tracks are likely to have linked these settlements.

In fact an easier and more direct route of a little over eight miles was available. If Oswald's men moved directly south from Heavenfield, over Fallowfield Fell and down the gently dropping track (today a tarmac lane) to Acomb, they would reach the site of the 'High Ford' across the Tyne in less than an hour. The river is broad here and shallow. In earlier days the ford passed over small

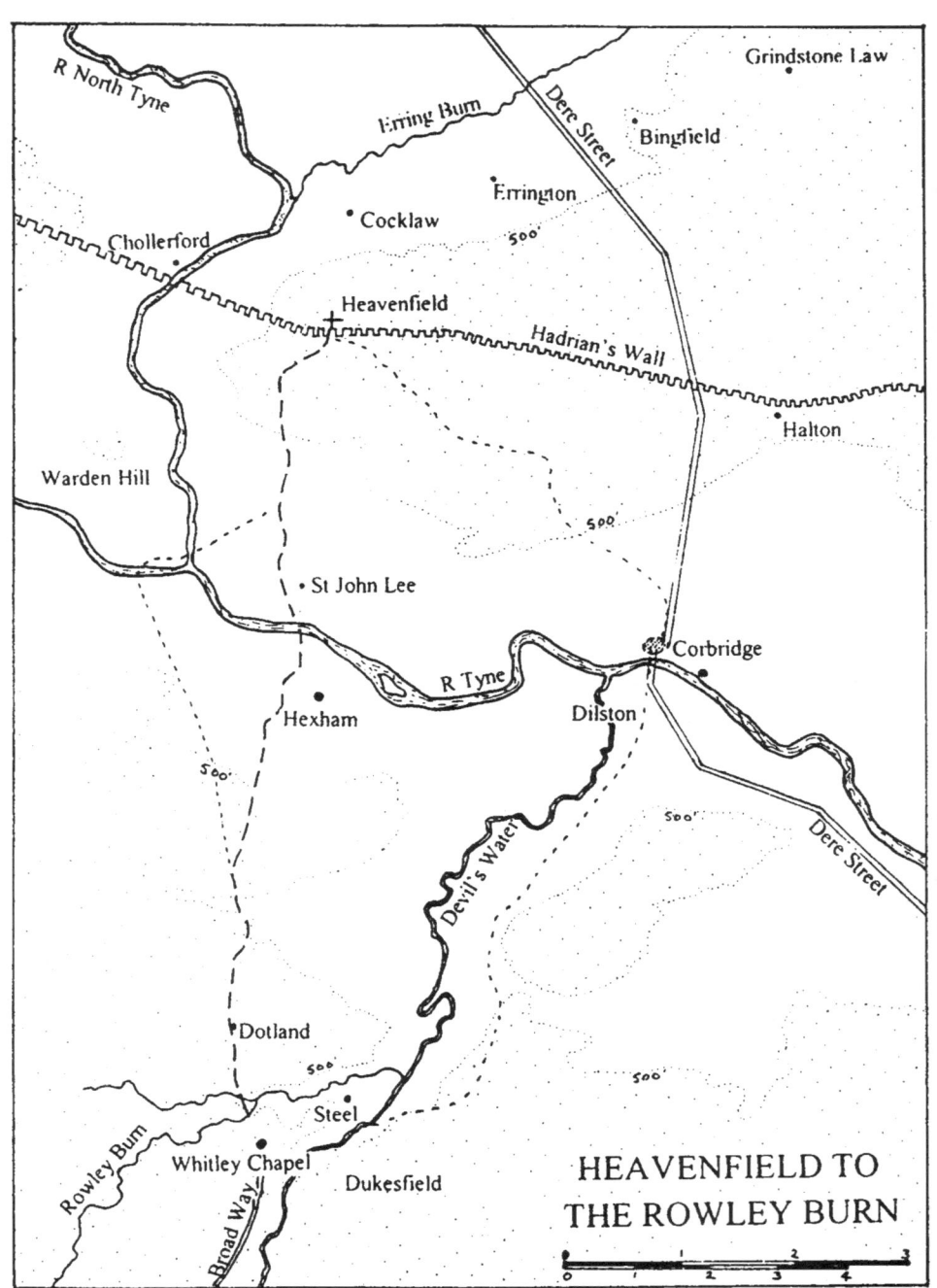

7. THE BATTLE OF HEAVENFIELD

islands and mudbanks. The crossing might be hazardous in darkness, but would be perfectly possible at first light if the river was at normal level. Tracks from the north still aim towards this point, though the modern road pattern ignores it; south of the river, Tyne Green Road follows an ancient direct approach. Along this line, Oswald's army would face a steady uphill march to Yarridge, followed by a relaxing downhill stretch to the crossing of West Dipton Burn near the present Dipton Mill. There was another climb to Dotland, and there the objective was exhilaratingly clear in front, though early morning mist might well hide the opposing forces from each other. From Dotland, a good path drops to the easy crossing of the Rowley Burn at Whitley Mill.

It is possible to walk this route today (including a minor deviation to cross the Tyne by the bridge instead of the ford) in about two hours and twenty minutes. Tarmac may make easier going than unmade tracks, but there were fewer such obstacles as stiles, gates, enclosures and speeding traffic. The route would bring Oswald's men out at the open end of the Whitley ridge. From Whitley Mill the ascent is easy to the Whitley Chapel Hill; or, if Cadwallon's unsuspecting men lay further to the east, on the cliffs overlooking the burn at Steel, they might face attack on an exposed flank. It would still be early in the day, with the Welsh perhaps sleeping off a good day of pillaging and ravaging. If the Northumbrians succeeded in surprising and driving back their enemies, Cadwallon's men would find themselves trapped between the converging valleys of the Burn and the Devil's Water. Neither stream is very large, but both cut deep into miniature gorges. A fast-moving attack might well have succeeded in driving Cadwallon and his whole army into the disaster that Bede implies.

The real problem of the battlefield is why and how Cadwallon came to be there in the first place. Cadwallon's base was in Deira. Oswald's might be expected to lie in his father's (and more recently his brother's) kingdom of Bernicia. Yet their meeting took place not on the line between York and the Yeavering-Bamburgh heartland of Bernicia but far to the west, in what later became Hexhamshire. It is difficult to understand what drew Cadwallon westward. If he was going west in pursuit of Oswald, why had the Northumbrian himself moved so far from his homeland?

Whitley is in the heart of the 'The Shire'. Hexhamshire, in medieval times the Regality of the Archbishop of York, is generally assumed to be identical with the *regio* granted about 670 to St Wilfrid by Queen Aethelthryth of Northumbria.

Hexhamshire may well have existed as a unit even before it became an Anglian royal estate. Its eastern boundary follows the Devil's Water, its northern lies in part along the Erring Burn; the former's name is certainly Celtic, the latter's may be, but no other names of early origin survive, except perhaps for Heavenfield itself and the Denisesburn. Bede's account implies that Heavenfield bore its English name even before 634; but his evidence is doubtful on this point, and the Denisesburn's name is, as explained above, of uncertain origin.

Hexhamshire has always been thinly peopled and relatively poor farming country. It is not easy to see why Cadwallon's army should have entered this remote area. The position is some six miles west of the main road to the north, the Dere Street, which Cadwallon could be expected to use if he was advancing

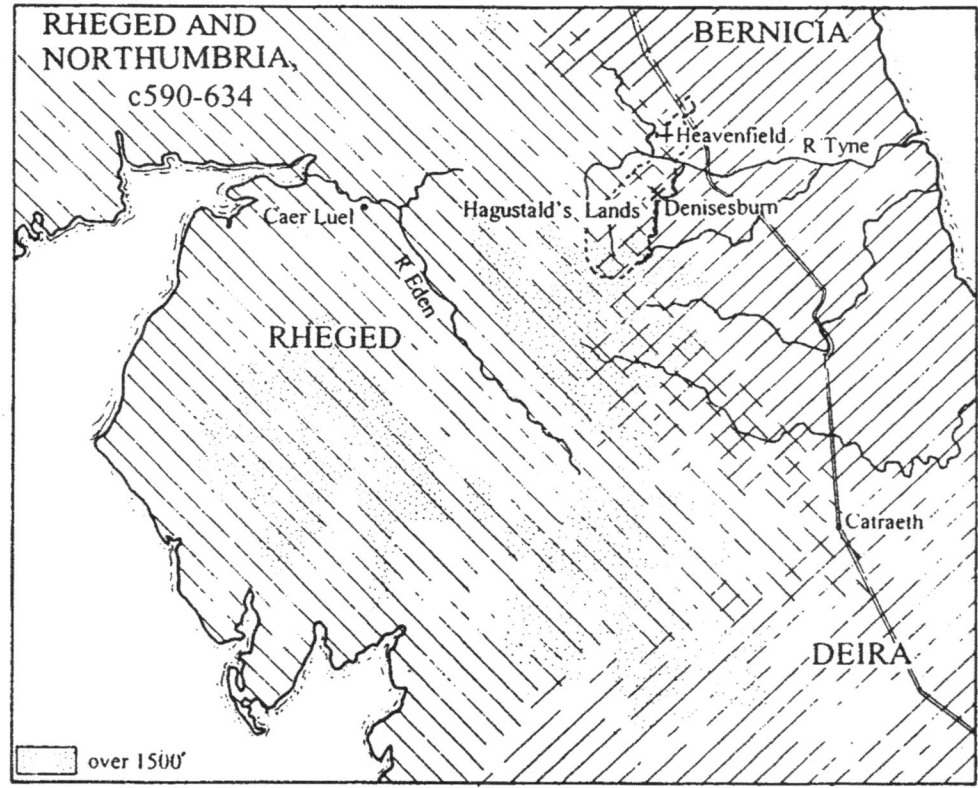

7. THE BATTLE OF HEAVENFIELD

from Deira (rather than from Cumbria, as Raine assumed). The 'Broad Way', a possible alternative approach, leads beyond Lilswood Moor only to the high Pennine wastes and the head of Allendale.

In the far west was the British kingdom of Rheged, whose extent is uncertain and probably fluctuated. Its great days of political and cultural supremacy had passed when its most celebrated ruler, Urien, was slain some time before 592. Urien seems to have headed a confederate kingdom, successor to the Brigantian tribal confederacy of Roman times. He occupied a leading place among the Celtic states whose territories stretched from the Forth-Clyde to the Trent, but Rheged's moment of triumph was brief. The bards who acclaimed its glory also sang its elegy. The fall of Rheged seems attributable to conflict among the Celts rather than with the Anglo-Saxon invaders; wars between British kings were as common as clashes between Celt and Saxon, or conflicts among the English kings themselves. With the death of Urien's warrior son Owain a few years later (perhaps about 595) Rheged virtually disappears from history (Jackson 1963 and Chadwick 1963, 32-3, 49-51, 156-9, 161-4; Morris 1973, 232-4, 284; Lovecy 1976, 34-45; Higham 1993, 82, 90; Cramp 1995). Aethelfrith, the all-conquering king of Bernicia, who slew his enemies to the north (at *Degsastan*) south (at Catterick) and south-west (at Chester) faced no known military problems upon his western border, and Rheged apparently continued as a quiescent client state. It was not, however, completely absorbed into the Northumbrian kingdom until Ecgfrith's reign, when the king handed over estates there to Wilfrid (Chadwick 1963, 42, 328-9; Kirby 1991 70, 90; Stancliffe & Cambridge 1995, 56-7).

The Rheged royal dynasty continued. Nennius's version of Rheged's history concludes with the marriage of Urien's great-granddaughter Riemmelth (Rhiainfellt) to Oswiu, the younger brother of King Oswald. This probably marked both the clinching of the alliance and a significant stage in the kingdom's absorption into Northumbria (Cramp 1995). Riemmelth's grandfather, Urien's scholarly son Rhun, plays so significant a part in the Welsh chronicles as to suggest that he may himself have been the original chronicler. The emphasis on his role in converting Northumbria underlined the cultural links between the two kingdoms. Rhun's son was Royth, the shadowy father of Riemmelth who may have been ruler of Rheged at the time of Heavenfield.

The bounds of Rheged as are uncertain as its status. The Solway estuary was at its heart, and its main centre seems to have been at sub-Roman Carlisle, though Urien also held court by the Lyvennet, in the Eden valley. Place-names suggest that Rheged stretched as far as Dunragit at the western end of Galloway, and to Rochdale at the southern end of Lancashire. There is no evidence at all about its eastward extent, except that it included the Eden valley and stretched 'into and perhaps to the far side of the Pennines', with 'Catraeth (Catterick in Yorkshire) as its south-eastern outpost' (Lovecy 1976, 37).

One might expect a subject people, British and Christian, to turn to Cadwallon as their champion. In fact, after some thirty years of apparently peaceful relations with Northumbria, Rheged seems to have regarded the Welsh advance as a danger. Oswiu's marriage confirmed a close relationship, and the Christian allegiance of the Northumbrian ruling dynasty. It may have taken place even before Heavenfield. Riemmelth's daughter was married to Peada of Mercia in

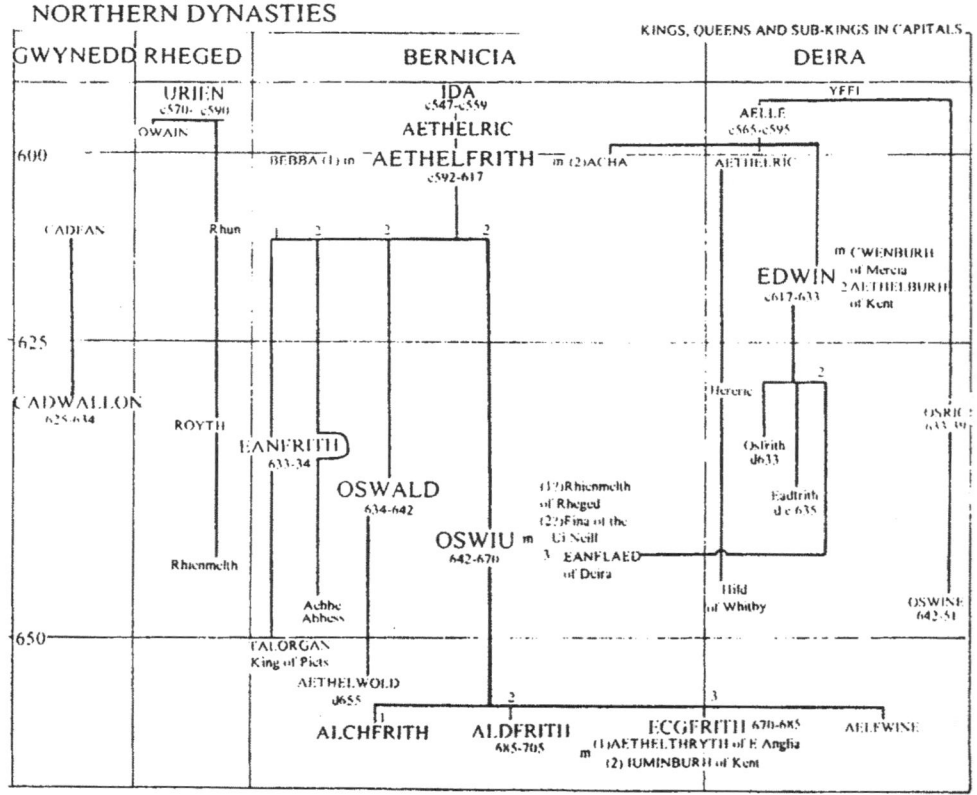

7. THE BATTLE OF HEAVENFIELD

the early 650s, while her son Alchfrith was active politically and militarily by 655; so her marriage to Oswiu may well have taken place twenty years before that time, while the Northumbrian prince was still in exile or at the moment of his return (Kirby 1991, 90).

If Oswald and his younger brother were reinforcing their links with Rheged, Cadwallon faced a threat from the west. Between Rheged and Dere Street, the road that linked Cadwallon's new conquests, lay a region of moorland and dales whose political geography and loyalties are unknown. Where the frontiers of Bernicia met those of Rheged is uncertain, if they met at all. In the middle of that region was what later became the royal estate of Hexhamshire. At least from early medieval times, the narrow valley of the Devil's Water marked very clearly the eastern boundary of the Shire. It may at some earlier time have formed the eastern border of Rheged. It was just west of the Devil's Water that Cadwallon apparently set up his camp.

Bede's account of the year preceding Heavenfield is relevant, though it was a year so ' hateful to all good men' that, regrettably, Bede did his best to wipe it from memory. He tells us that the three sons of Aethelfrith were allowed to return to Bernicia after the death of Edwin; perhaps this was their reward for collaborating with Cadwallon against their uncle. Nevertheless Cadwallon spent a year in the Northumbrian kingdoms, 'ravaging them like a savage tyrant'. Eanfrith, his puppet king of Bernicia, reacted by trying to stir up Saxon paganism against his overlord, but this betrayal of their shared faith only infuriated Cadwallon; the apostasy was as despicable for him as it seemed later to Bede. When Eanfrith came with his thegns seeking peace, Cadwallon slew them. This was the immediate prelude to the Heavenfield campaign against Eanfrith's younger brothers, Oswald and Oswiu, who were presumably also back in home territory, though perhaps not in Bernicia. In fact they were probably not far from where they were shortly to meet Cadwallon's army, somewhere in the later Hexhamshire.

Bede, a century later, knew the abbey founded by Wilfrid in Hexhamshire, the *regio* (or estate) given him by the queen of Northumbria, as *Ecclesia Hagustaldensis,* 'The Hagustaldian Church' (Colgrave & Mynors 1969, 216). The earliest English form of Hexhamshire's name is *Hagustaldes ea,* the Hagustald's 'island'. Hagustald, which later in its Northumbrian dialect form *hehstald* gave the medieval form Hestoldesham, has been variously translated as a young warrior, a landless younger son, or a (male or female) virgin. It is used in this last sense by the Northumbrian glossator of the Lindisfarne Gospels to translate *Virgo*. Bede probably knew, though he does not bother to tell us, the identity of the first lord of the hagustaldian estate, from whom its name derived. Possibilities include the two known holders of the estate: Aethelthryth, the queen who preserved her virginity throughout her marriage and gave the territory to Wilfrid; and the saintly bishop himself, a landless Northumbrian nobleman who became a churchman. Both of these, however, seem to be ruled out by the British version of the name; *scaul* is best translated as 'young warrior' (Jackson 1963, 34).

Another possible candidate for the role of hagustald is Oswald, who, in the year while his elder half-brother was puppet king of Bernicia might have been allotted a territory on the fringe of Rheged; we might know more of this but for the fact that Bede regarded Oswald as rightful king throughout the year of the apostate. But it is Oswald's younger brother, still a landless younger son after Heavenfield, who has perhaps the best claim of all (Watts 1995; Corfe 1991). For the Britons of Rheged, he was the young warrior who had married their princess, and perhaps the bargain was sealed by transfer of this border territory. Another possibility is that there was a succession of hagustalds, with the 'hagustaldian' land as a fiefdom for someone close to the throne, rather in the manner of the 'Duchy' lands of Cornwall in later times. If we assume that Oswald or Oswiu acquired the estate on the occasion of the Rheged marriage, perhaps as a dowry for Oswiu's bride, it would pass in time to Oswiu's younger son Ecgfrith while his half-brother Alchfrith was sub-king of Deira, and then as a wedding portion to Ecgfrith's wife Aethelthryth; who chose however, to alienate it to Wilfrid.

Cadwallon probably slew Eanfrith in the early autumn of 634 (Wood 1983, 288); though the 1927 cross at Heavenfield prefers 635, as does the later information board (it grants that some scholars favour 633). Presumably, having effectively destroyed resistance in Bernicia, Cadwallon had to face Oswald and Oswiu operating from their own newly acquired territorial base on the frontiers of their Rheged ally. It is likely that when Cadwallon advanced westward from Dere Street he was not pursuing Oswald's army through the tangle of little valleys but rather seeking a firm base from which to ravage, in his customary fashion, the hagustald's territory and the Rheged frontier. Crossing the frontier line of the Devil's Water he arrived in the Whitley area just beyond, which may well have been the focal point on a north-south route binding the Shire together, from the Tyne ford through Dotland to the Broad Way. From this centre

7. THE BATTLE OF HEAVENFIELD

Cadwallon would proceed to the kind of savage activity which Bede regularly attributes to him.

Oswald could be expected to withdraw behind the Tyne, to set up his battle standard at some clearly defined and named spot where supporters might gather by major roads from Bernicia in the east, Scotland in the north, and Rheged in the west; at Heavenfield, in fact. If Oswald knew that his enemy was operating from a fixed base, the king could plan his dawn advance confident of where to find and surprise Cadwallon.

If we can accept the rather inadequate evidence locating Cadwallon's disaster on the Rowley Burn, the geography of 'the Battle of Heavenfield' has been clear since Raine's publication in the 1860s, however much his simultaneous flight of imagination helped to perpetuate the confusion that still exists. The battle's location poses problems to which there are no clearcut solution; though it seems likely that the continued existence of Rheged not far off and of the Hagustald's Lands close by may be significant.

REFERENCES

Alcock L 1971 *Arthur's Britain, History and Archaeology AD367-634*, Penguin.

Anderson A O & Anderson M O, ed and trans 1961 *Adomnan's Life of Columba* Nelson

Chadwick N K ed 1963 *Celt and Saxon, Studies in the Early British Border* Cambridge University Press

Colgrave B & Mynors R A B, ed and trans 1969 *Bede's Ecclesiastical History of the English People* Oxford, Clarendon

Corfe T 1991 'How Hexham got its name' *Hexham Historian* 1, 43-48

Coulson W 1861 'Denisesburn' *Archaeologia Aeliana* 2nd series, V, 103-8

Cramp R 1995 *Whithorn and the Northumbrian Expansion Westwards* Whithorn

Eagles J 1991 *Landscape and Community: a World Heritage Site in rural Northumberland*, unpublished M Litt thesis, Newcastle; copy held by Wall LHS

Ekwall E 1960 *The Oxford Dictionary of English Place-Names*, 4th ed, Oxford University Press

Greenwell W 1863-4 'Address to the Members' *Transactions of the Tyneside Naturalists Field Club*, vol VI, 1-30

Higham N J 1993 *The Kingdom of Northumbria, AD350-1100* Alan Sutton

Hodgkin T 1906 *The History of England from the Earliest Times to the Norman Conquest* Longmans, Green

Hodgon J 1840 *History of Northumberland* Part II, vol III, Newcastle, for the author

Hodgson J C 1897 *Northumberland County History, Vol IV, Hexhamshire Part 2,* Newcastle, Andrew Reid

Hunter Blair P 1970 *The World of Bede* Secker & Warburg

Hutchinson W 1778 *A view of Northumberland...* Newcastle

Jackson K 1963 'On the North British Section of Nennius' in Chadwick ed 1963

Kirby D P 1991 *The Earliest English Kings* Unwin & Hyman

Lovecy I 1976 'The end of Celtic Britain: a sixth-century battle near Lindisfarne' *Archaeologia Aeliana* 5th Series, IV, 31-45

Mackenzie E 1811 *An Historical and Descriptive View of the County of Northumberland...* Mackenzie & Dent

Mackenzie E 1825 *An Historical, Topographical and Descriptive View of the County of Northumberland...* Newcastle

Morris J 1973 *The Age of Arthur* Weidenfeld & Nicolson

Plummer C ed 1896 *Venerabilis Baedae Opera Historica* Oxford University Press

Raine J ed 1864 *The Priorty of Hexham...* Surtees Society 44

Sadler J 1988 *Battle for Northumbria* Morpeth, Bridge Studios

Selkirk R 1995 *On the Trail of the Legions* Ipswich, Anglia Publishing

Stancliffe C & Cambridge E eds 1995 *Oswald, Northumbrian King to European Saint* Stamford, Paul Watkins

Stenton F M 1943 *Anglo-Saxon England* Oxford University Press

Sykes J 1833 *Local Records; or Historical Register...* Newcastle

Thacker A 1995 'Membra Disjecta' in Stancliffe & Cambridge eds 1995, 97-127

Toulmin Smith L ed 1906-1910 *The Itinerary of John Leland in or about the years 1535-1543*, reprint 1964

Wallis W J 1769 *The Natural History and Antiquities of Northumberland...* London

Watts V E 1995 'The Place-name Hexham' *Hexham Historian* 5, 4-5

Watts V E 1996 personal communication 11/01/96

Wood S 1983 'Bede's Northumbrian Dates Again' in *English Historical Review,* XCVIII, 280-96

Acknowledgements

I am grateful for help from Roy Berrill, Meg Burdon, Eric Cambridge, Rosemary Cramp, Colin and Marjorie Dallison, Constance Fraser, Ralph Kaner, Liz Sobell, Victor Watts.

8. HEXHAM BEFORE WILFRID?

There are those who find thirteen centuries of history not quite enough. Six more centuries would honour Hexham with Roman roots. Many well-informed and sensible people are quite sure that those roots are waiting to be found. Was the seventh-century Hagustaldian abbey constructed not only from re-used Roman stones but on a re-used Roman site? Eighteenth-century antiquarians favoured the possibility, and enthusiasts have been hunting for proof ever since. But there have always been others to throw cold water on the notion. Three centuries of investigation and debate have not resolved the issue.

William Stukeley and John Horsley wrote soon after the discovery in 1725 of the Abbey crypt. They marvelled at the dedication to Septimius Severus and his sons built into its roof (Collingwood & Wright 1965, no 1151). 'These stones and inscriptions', wrote Horsley,

> argue Hexham to have been a Roman station... And this might have been a town in the Roman times... Having elsewhere proved that it is not *Axelodunum*, I know not what name to give it, unless we suppose it to have been Ptolemy's *Epiacum*.

Horsley was duly quoted at length in the first history of Hexham (Wright 1823, 119-131). Wright carefully set out the arguments on both sides of what was already a long-running debate, and judiciously suggested that 'the intelligent reader may draw his own conclusions.'

The debate was given fresh impetus in the middle of the nineteenth century. In 1857 Joseph Fairless, a Hexham builder with a lively and acquisitive interest in antiquities, recorded that

> In cutting a drain through the Hall Gate Hexham the Workmen came upon some ancient water pipes of hard burnt clay of curious construction about four feet below the surface. The jointing lengths were about sixteen inches, one end enlarged in funnel shape to receive the compressed end of the joining pipe, the diameter about 2¾ inches they seem to be hand formed in make with a deep <u>screw threaded interior</u> of novel description and as perfect

in durability, as when they were taken from the Kiln. There are Roman clay pipes at the Chesters of the same construction. Query can these be Roman (Fairless, 8th July 1857).

Paul Bidwell has traced the sequel. Dr John Collingwood Bruce, a formidable expert, came forward as champion of the Roman case. During a country meeting of the Society of Antiquaries of Newcastle-upon-Tyne on 15th August 1860, Dr Bruce set out 'the various considerations which tend to show that Hexham itself was a Roman town' (1861, 145-7). Apart from 'the early greatness of Hexham' and its position 'just such as the Romans would choose', certain direct proofs were cited: first, the crypt of the Abbey was composed wholly of Roman stones; secondly, by the Manor Office Mr Fairless had recently 'found a connected chain of earthenware pipes of manifest Roman workmanship, lying *in situ.*' Bruce (1863, 85), in the first edition of his *Handbook to the Roman Wall* (originally *The Wallet Book...*), described Hexham as a Roman fort. In later editions this identification was qualified, until R G Collingwood removed from his ninth edition (1933) any mention of Hexham as a Roman site. This was in part a result of the excavations at Corbridge before the First World War, when that site was revealed to be extensive enough to supply all the Roman stones re-used at Hexham. But the conversion of the *Handbook* did not end the debate. From time to time it flares up afresh in press or publication, usually generating more heat than light.

Some of the arguments have already been put forward in earlier chapters. It is time to bring them together.

First, no Roman text or inscription refers to a site that can be identified as Hexham. Where the geography of Roman Tynedale as a whole is well documented in the *Antonine Itinerary*, the *Ravenna Cosmography*, and the *Notitia Dignitatum*, and a great many places on and near the Wall or on main roads are named in these sources, none of them can be located at Hexham. Several dedications appear on stones found at Hexham, but none gives a place-name. Early antiquaries identified Hexham as either the *Axelodunum* of the *Notitia* or the *Epiacum* of Ptolemy; but the former, as Horsley argued, is now assumed to be at the western end of the Wall, either Stanwix or Netherby, and the latter is probably Whitley Castle (Jones & Mattingly 1990, 16-42; Rivet & Smith 1979, 360, 483).

Second, no structural remains in the town area can be identified as Roman. The numerous foundations seen in and around the Abbey during the nineteenth

8. HEXHAM BEFORE WILFRID?

century all seem to be related to the succession of churches there from Wilfrid's day. Dowsing has suggested a possible quadruple fort ditch in the Abbey Grounds (Selkirk 1995, 309-10), but this has not been confirmed. It may be noted that, on the evidence of topographical remains and air photography, there must be few places in Tynedale that were not at some time or other occupied by a temporary Roman encampment, as is evident on the opposite bank of the Tyne. Geophysical surveys in the vicinity of the Abbey have so far revealed only extreme confusion beneath the surface. The most potentially positive evidence is that of Joseph Fairless's chain of water-pipes, found beneath what was once a busy approach to medieval Hexham. Expert opinion is almost universally, if cautiously, sceptical of a Roman date. Many similar pipes are known; some certainly come from the medieval period (eg Allan 1984, fig 49, nos 1515-30); fig 77, no 1774), and others can be dated to any century from the first to the eighteenth. It is unlikely, but just possible, that the Hexham pipes might constitute real evidence of a Roman water system, but only scientific analysis by thermoluminescent testing could resolve that issue.

Third, there is no question but that an enormous quantity of Roman stone was used and re-used in the course of building early Hexham. The Abbey crypt is wholly constructed from Roman stones. A number bear deep-cut decoration, friezes or lewis holes, most show cross-broaching, and there are two dedications. The one that so impressed Horsley was set up originally to Septimius Severus, probably on the eve of his Scottish campaign in AD 207-8; it celebrated the erection of a new granary, presumably at Corbridge. The other was on an altar to Apollo (Collingwood & Wright 1965, no 1122). A third, also recorded by Horsley but now lost, included a reference to the otherwise unknown Corionototae (no 1142). Further altars and stones, with or without inscriptions, have been found at various times in and around the Abbey, especially during the construction of Beaumont Street in 1864. Later buildings, such as the Old Gaol of 1330-2, obviously include Roman material, perhaps re-using it for the second or third time. The massive Flavinus memorial stone (no 1172) was found in 1881 laid face down in a (probably twelfth-century) foundation wall, and raised the problem of why it should remain awkwardly intact if the only purpose in bringing it to Hexham was for building stone.

It is generally assumed that most of this material derives, like the Severus inscription, from Corbridge; from sculpturally decorated houses in the civil settlement, from the massive building blocks of the bridge, from the military cemetery and associated shrines. M D King has argued that the seven fragments of leaf-and-berry frieze, and the pieces of fluted pilaster (all re-used in the crypt) were originally part of the interior decorative scheme in the third-century western headquarters building. Redundant and ruinous, it would have been finally demolished when good quality material was needed by Wilfrid's workmen. This scenario might explain why no closely matching fragments have been found at the Corbridge site (King 1988, 19-27, 92). The discovery of several stones from Corbridge in the river near the present Hexham bridge has been taken to imply an accident during transportation by raft or by waggon and ford (Hinds 1896, 240). Though such a wealth of stone might seem to suggest an urban settlement and a cemetery closer than Corbridge, the enormous building effort made under Wilfrid and his successors, by Anglo-Saxon workmen totally unfamiliar with quarrying techniques, makes if likely that ready-made material would be eagerly sought and brought from wherever it was readily available.

Fourth, and in remarkable contrast to the wealth of Roman stone, there seems to be an almost complete absence of occupation evidence from small finds. No metalware other than a stray coin, no glassware, above all no pottery has appeared during frequent excavations in the town centre area. Any intensive or lasting settlement, military or civil, would certainly leave such traces.

Fifth, Ray Selkirk has proposed a road network on the south side of the Tyne that seems to focus on Hexham Abbey. Its main components are (i) Ebchester-Hexham, taking a direct line from the point at Apperley Dene where the known Dere Street bends northward; (ii) 'Forster's Road', from Dilston, another link from Dere Street westward; this is the line followed by the medieval 'Delegate' that gave its name to a house south-east of Hexham; (iii) A '255° Frontier' road which follows a line ruled from the North Sea at St. Mary's Island to a fortlet on the Cumbrian Irish Sea coast, by way of Hexham and Staward Peel (Selkirk 1995, 304-14); (iv) another line ruled from the Dotland DMV site (NY 923 595) to a crossing of the South Tyne near Burnfoot (NY 905 658) misses the Abbey (Selkirk 1995, 126-9); (v) the modern Dipton Mill to Hexham road seems for part of its length to be aligned on the Abbey, and this alignment apparently continues along field boundaries and the nineteenth-century path sometimes called 'The Pilgrim's Way'. Selkirk has made impressive field observations, and it seems likely that there were early roads on at least some of these routes; but there has been no verification by excavation or independent observation, and the whole proposal remains dubious.

Finally, the likelihood that a military or civil settlement might develop on the

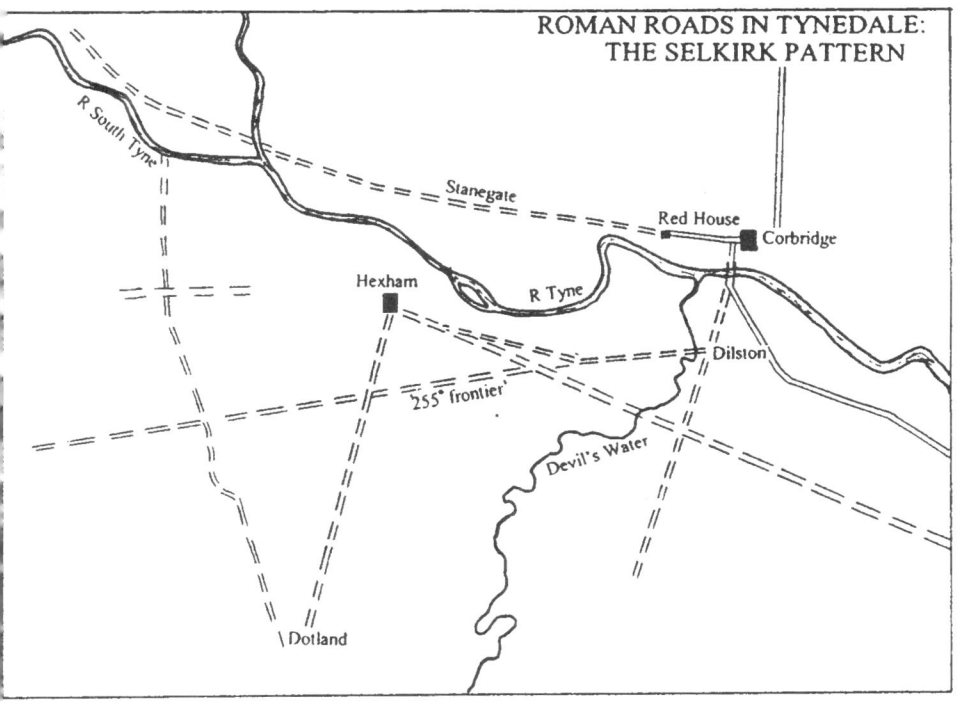

site of Hexham has to be considered. The site seems strategically and tactically appropriate. It is set on a prominent bluff overlooking the river at a point just below the confluence, where the east-west valley route meets another from the north. Close to the bluff the river is shallow and dotted with sandbanks and islands that make fording it quite possible, though occasionally hazardous. There is no question that an important fort, later a major supply base with an extensive civil settlement, existed throughout the Roman period less than three miles away on the other side of the river. It seems doubtful that any other significant focus of settlement would come into existence so near. Moreover, Roman lines of communication, particularly the Stanegate, all prefer the north side of the Tyne. It remains a possibility that in the early stages of the occupation invading forces may have used some of the routes suggested by Selkirk and occupied temporarily the terrace above the valley, where there was probably already an enclosed native settlement on Windmill Hill. But it is difficult to see what circumstances might bring into existence on that site a permanent stone-built fort (such as those beside the Stanegate or on the Wall), or a substantial stone-built town in any way resembling Corbridge.

There is no archaeological evidence for Roman Hexham. Equally, there is none for any occupation of the site during the post-Roman period, or at any time before Wilfrid's arrival. But given the general inadequacy of the archaeological record for these centuries, in stark contract to the rich legacy of the Roman occupation, this cannot be taken as proof that there was nothing at Hexham before Wilfrid's arrival. Rosemary Cramp (above, p 64) has suggested that the topography of Hexham might have suited a sixth-century petty ruler or local war-lord. Its prominent and defensible site, as well as its frontier setting and its domination of a major east-west route, combine to make Hexham a likely stronghold and administrative centre. Peter Ryder (1994) has pointed out that Wilfrid's failure to plant his abbey on the prime site at the eastern end of the Hexham terrace implies that there was already a significant building there, an administrative centre for the estate he had been granted or even (since the estate was the queen's) a royal hall. The Seal, whose name first occurs about 1215 as 'Sele' (Raine 1865, 90), also suggests the Old English *sele*, a hall, another possible early centre.

If a stronghold or a hall existed in the seventh century, then it was the central place of the region that Aethelthryth gave Wilfrid. It has been long assumed that the *regio* was an earlier manifestation of the medieval Hexhamshire. Since the 1960s the work of G R J Jones on 'multiple estates' in Wales and Yorkshire (1976 etc), and that of Geoffrey Barrow on 'shires' in southern Scotland and northern England has taught us to expect such administrative and economic units to have their roots in the Celtic past (1973; also Smith 1983 and Gregson 1983). Hexhamshire is likely to have been just such an old-established territorial unit. It may well have faced across the Tyne another similar unit that had its high place at Warden, whose hill-fort, Saxon remains, early motte, and extensive parish all suggest ancient importance. Hexhamshire, within whose bounds so much happened in 634 (above, p 83-5) may have been a frontline territory of the kingdom of Rheged that changed hands around 634. In any version of events, Aethelthryth's gift is unlikely to have been in English hands for very long before she transferred it to Wilfrid.

It is reasonable to assume that, despite the complete lack of archaeological evidence, the territory that ultimately became Hexhamshire came into being under native British rulers. Perhaps these were the kings of the North Britons, the lords of Rheged; or possibly the land's origin lay even further back in the time of the Brigantes. Whenever such a territorial unit came into being, it was administered from a central place which is most likely to have been where Hexham was later built.

REFERENCES

Allan J P 1984 *Medieval and Post-Medieval Finds from Exeter, 1971-1980* (*Exeter Archaeological Report 3*), Exeter.

Barrow G W S 1973 'Pre-feudal Scotland: Shires and Thanes', in *The Kingdom of the Scots, 7-68*; London, Arnold.

Bruce J C 1861 'Roman Hexham' *Archaeologia Aeliana*, 2nd series V, 144-7.

Bruce J C 1863 *The Wallet-Book of the Roman Wall*, Newcastle upon Tyne.

Clack P & Ivy J eds 1983 *The Borders*, Durham, CBA Group 3.

Collingwood R G 1933 *The Handbook of the Roman Wall* (9th ed) Newcastle upon Tyne, Andrew Reid.

Fairless J (1789-1873), *Table Book*, Ms privately owned, transcriptions by Colin Dallison.

Gregory N 1983 'The Multiple Estate Model', 49-79 in Clack & Ivy 1983.

Jones G R J 1976 'Multiple Estates and Early Settlement' 15-40, in Sawyer P H ed *Medieval Settlement*, London, Arnold.

King M D 1988, *Sources and Influences: a Study of the Roman and Anglian Architectural Sculpture of Hexham Abbey*, unpublished MA dissertation, Durham.

Raine J, 1865 *The Priory of Hexham, vol II: Its title deeds, Black Book* etc Surtees Soc 46.

Smith I M 1983 'Brito-Roman and Anglo-Saxon: the Unification of the Borders' in Clack & Ivy 1983, 9-48.

Wright A B 1823 *An Essay towards a History of Hexham...* Alnwick, Davison.

INDEX

Adomnan 71, 75-6
Aethelfrith, King 62, 81, 83
Aethelthryth (Etheldreda), Queen 5, 8, 64, 79, 83-4, 92
Agricola, Cn Julius 6, 11, 14, 20
air Photography 8, 52, 89
Ala Petriana 11, 14
Allen, R 13, 22
Allendale 13, 14, 74, 81
altars, Roman 12, 15-6, 22, 89
Anglo-Saxons 8, 12, 41, 43, 45, 49, 52, 57, 59-60, 62, 90; invasion of 57, 61-3
antiquarians 21-2, 87
Antiquaries, Soc of (Newcastle 68, 88)
Antonine Wall 15, 24, 26
Apollo, dedications to 6, 15, 89
Apperley Dene, RB farm 15-6, 90
Armstrong map 46-7
auxiliary troops, Roman 11, 14, 29
Axellodunum 87-8
Barcombe Hill 13
Bede 5, 8, 59, 65-6, 69-76, 79-80, 83; *Ecclesiastical History* of, quoted 71-2, 74-5
Bernicia (*Bernaccia, Berneich*) 8, 57, 59-64, 76, 79, 83, 85
Bidwell, P 6, 18-28, 56, 88
Binchester fort 32-3
Birdoswald (*Banna*) 7, 29-37, 61; granaries at, 30-2, 36; post-Roman, 30-36, 61
Bishop Rigg 48
bridges 18, 21-3, 25-7; abutments 26, 42; at Bywell 23; at Chesters 25-7; at Corbridge 26-7, 41-3; dating of 26; Roman 42; at Willowford, 25
Brigantes 5, 13, 20, 93
Brigomaglos (inscription) 7, 33
Britain, Roman 11, 20
Broad Way 74, 81, 84
Bronze Age 13
brooches, late Roman and Anglo-Saxon 59, 62
Broomhouse Common, settlement site 10, 14
Brougham 61

Bruce, J Collingwood 88
burial customs 58-9, 61-2
Bywell 12, 22-3, 63
Cadbury Castle 31-2, 35-7
Cadwallon (Cadwalla), King of Gwynedd 65-6, 68-72, 74, 76-7, 79-81, 83-5
Ca(n)tscaul (Hexham) 76, 84
Carelgate 21, 42, 44, 48-9, 52
Carlisle 11, 14, 20-1, 24, 34, 42, 61, 64, 81
Catterick (Catraeth) 8, 18, 59, 62, 81, 82
Chesterholm (see Vindolanda) 12
Chesters, fort and museum 7, 12, 16, 25-8, 88; bridge, 25-7
Christianity 7-8, 34, 57-8, 61-3, 65, 76, 82
churches 34, 63; Corbridge 12-3, 51; Heavenfield, St. Oswald 12, 65-9, 73; Hexham 27, 52, 83
cist burials 13, 59, 68
Collingwood, R G 88
Columba, St, vision 71
Corbridge (*Coria, Coriosopitum*) 6-7, 11-4, 16, 19, 21-4, 26-8, 32, 40-7, 49, 55, 59, 64, 77, 89-90; bridge, Roman 26-7, 40-1, 47, 52, 55; bridges, later 51; excavations at 88; importance of 45, 55; mill 40-2, 48-9; Roman site 6, 42, 90; town 42
Cor Burn 42, 44, 47-9
Corchester (Colchester) Fields 42, 48-52
Corionototae 5, 89
Coventina 15
Cowderys Down 31
Cramp R 8, 57-64, 92
Crow J G 6, 11-7
Cumbria 8, 20, 69, 81
Deira 57, 60, 62-3, 76, 79, 84
deities, native and Roman 6, 15
Delegate Hall 90
Denisesburn 65-6, 68, 70, 72-3, 76
Dere Street 11-2, 14-5, 20, 23, 42, 49, 51-2, 59, 64, 80, 83-4, 90
Devil's Water 8, 21, 42, 73-4, 78-80, 83-4
Dilston 21, 51, 90

Doon Hill 32
Dotland 79, 84, 90
dowsing 89
Durham, 20, 59-60, 64
'eales' 49-52
Eanfrith 76, 83-4
Ebchester 15
Ecgfrith, King 8, 81, 84
Eden, R and valley 20-1, 81-2
Edwin, King 83
Edge House settlement 10, 14
Epiacum 87-8
Erring Burn 65, 68, 72-4, 80
Fairless J 87-9
Fallowfield 73, 77
farming 5, 6, 13-4, 32-3, 77
Flavinus 11, 14, 89
foederati 60
Forster RH 41-2, 49
forts, Roman 11, 14, 21, 23-4, 29, 33-5, 37-8, 60-1
frontier troops *(limitanei)* 29-30, 34-7
frontiers 6, 11, 21, 35, 38, 63-4, 92; Stanegate as, 21; 255*, 90; Tyne-Solway, 11, 59-60; Tyne Valley as 63-4; Dere St, 59, 63
Fryer J, maps of 46-8
Gildas 36, 59
Gillam, John 41
glassware, Roman 15-6, 90
Greenwell W 73
Hadrian 11, 23-4; and see Wall
hagustald, Hagustald's Lands 83-5, 92; *hagustaldes-ea* 63, 77, 83
Hartleyburn Common 14
Heavenfield, accounts of, 65-72; battle of 8, 65-86; church, 12, 65, 67-9, 73, 75; cross at 65-7, 69, 73-6; miracles, 75; name, 75; notice board 67; pilgrimage 66, 75; site, 66-8;
Hexham 6-7, 13, 56, 63-6, 69, 87-93; Abbey 11, 14-7, 27, 52, 72, 74, 83, 87, 90; crypt, 11, 88, 90; monks of, 71, 74-5; name of, 8, 77, 83; possible origins of, 6-7, 16, 87-93; Windmill Hill, 13, 91

Hexhamshire 5, 42, 64, 72, 74, 79-80, 83-4, 92; origins, 8, 92-3
hill-forts 5, 13, 35, 60
Historia Brittonum (Nennius) 76
Hodgson J 22, 68
Hodgson J C, quoted 70
Horsley, J 21-2, 24, 87, 89
hunters, prehistoric 13
Hutchinson W 65-6
inscriptions 38, 63, 68
Iona 71, 76
Iron Age 5, 13-4
islands, at Corbridge 43-52
Jarrow 63
Jobey G 15-6
King M D 89-90
Latin 7, 57-8, 63, 73
limitanei, see frontier troops
Lindisfarne (Holy Island) 63-4, 84
literacy 63
Maiden Way 21
Maponus 6, 15
maps, of Corbridge area 43, 45-9
'Men of the North' 77
Mesolithic 13
metallurgy 61, 63
Milfield 32, 62
Military Way (Roman) 12, 24-7
Military Road (18th C) 65
mills, see watermills
Monkwearmouth 59
Mote of Mark 60-2
Ninian, St 61
North Britons 77
Northumberland County Council 41, 56, 67-8
Northumberland County History 16, 40, 49, 51, 70
Northumbria 5, 8, 37, 59, 81
Notitia Dignitatum 30, 88
Old Town, Allendale 22
Ordnance Survey 45, 47-8
Oswald, King 65-72, 74-6, 83-5
Oswiu, King 81-4

Palaeolithic 13
Passmore D 47, 52, 56
Patrick, St 7, 61
Picts 33, 57, 60, 63
Piercebridge 19, 32-3;
Piercebridge Formula, The 19
pipes, water, Roman 87-9
place-names as evidence, 5, 8, 12, 49, 52, 58-9, 72-3, 80-3
Portgate 23
pottery, Roman 15-6, 26, 34-5, 37, 61, 90
Procopius quoted 34-5
Prudhoe 13
Ptolemy 87-8
quays 19, 41
querns 14
radiocarbon dating 41, 61
Raine J 66, 68-70, 73, 85
Red House Burn 42, 44-5, 47-8, 52; fort, 6, 11, 14, 20-1
religion, Romano-British 6, 15, 22
Rheged, kingdom of 8, 61, 63-4, 67-7, 81-5
Rhienmelth (Rhiemmelth, Rhiainfellt) 81-4, 92
Rhun map Urien 81
Ripon 11
river transport 19
roads, Roman 6, 12, 18-27, 77, 90
Roecliffe fort 20-1
Roman Britain 10, 29-30, 32, 57; buildings, 12; conquest, 6, 11, 20; geographers, 88; in Tynedale, 5-6, 10, 22; roads, 6, 11, 18-27, 77, 90; taxes, 30, 36; withdrawal, 7, 29-32, 57
Romanisation 29-30, 36, 57
Rowley Burn 66, 70, 73-4, 77-9, 85; see Denisesburn
Ryder P F 8, 92
Scotland 11, 14-5, 24, 33, 59, 69, 76, 85
Selkirk R 6, 19, 21-3, 77, 90-1
Septimius Severus 26, 87, 89
shires 92
Snape, M 7, 28, 40-56

South Shields 34
Stanegate 11, 12, 14, 21, 23-7, 49, 52, 92
Stanwick 20
Staward Peel 12-3, 16-7, 22, 90
Stukeley W 87
supplies, military 18, 30, 32
Textoverdi 5, 13
timber building 31-2, 34, 36, 52, 61, 63
Thirlings 32, 63
tribes 7, 36, 57
Tyne, R 5, 7, 13-4, 16, 23, 25-7, 40-44, 49, 60, 69, 72-3, 77, 85, 89; erosion, 41-2, 43, 45; floods, 43, 47; fords, 14, 41, 51, 77; islands, 43, 46-9, 52; valley, 11, 49, 60, 61-4
Tynedale 5, 7-9, 11-4, 18, 20, 23, 29, 88
Tyne-Solway route 11, 20-1, 59-61, 63-4
Urien, king 81
Vallum 23-4, 70
vici 6, 16, 29
Vindolanda 6-7, 11, 13-4, 16-8, 21-3, 32-3; writing-tablets, 6, 13, 18
Votadini 5, 57
Wall, Hadrian's 5-6, 11, 14, 21, 23-6, 29, 32-8, 57, 59-60, 66-70, 77, 80
Wallsend 11, 30, 59
Warden 63-4, 92; hillfort, 5, 13, 61, 92
watermills 52-4; Anglo-Saxon, 27, 42, 45; at Corbridge, 27, 40-1, 43-4, 52-5; Tamworth, 45, 53, 55
water-pipes, ?Roman 87-9
West Heslerton 61-2
Whitfield 10, 14-5, 22
Whithorn 32
Whitley Castle 21, 88
Whitley Chapel 74, 79, 84
Wilfrid, St 5, 7-9, 11, 17, 52, 64, 75, 79, 81, 83-4, 90, 92
Wilmott T 7, 29-39
Wroxeter 31-2
Yeavering 8, 31, 62-3, 79
York 11, 33, 37, 61; Archbishops of, 73, 79